Chocolates, Sweets
& Toffees

Chocolates, Sweets & Toffees

Jan Morgan

with additional material by Rosemary Wadey

Photographs by Anthony Kay
Line drawings by Moira Shippard

Ward Lock Limited · London

Contents

Making Sweets

BOILING SUGAR

As all sweets have a high sugar content, their success depends on the boiling of the sugar. One degree too high or too low could spoil the texture and flavour of the whole batch.

Ideally, sweets should be made in a dry atmosphere. If it is damp, boiled sweets and toffees become sticky and chocolates will have a bloom on them (see Glossary).

Sugar syrups can be made in *heavy* pans on any type of cooker – gas, electric or solid fuel. The point to remember is that, whatever form of heat is used, the syrup *must* boil rapidly or the sweets will be sticky.

Making A Sugar Syrup

1. Take a clean, heavy saucepan. If the amount of syrup to be made is small, then use a small pan.

2. Dissolve the sugar in the water over a very low heat until every crystal has dissolved. Stir the syrup very gently with a *metal* tablespoon so that you can see when the sugar crystals have dissolved completely.

3. Once the sugar has dissolved, bring the syrup rapidly to the boil. Do not stir again as crystals may form and cause the sugar to revert to an opaque mass. If crystals *do* begin to form around the sides of the pan, very carefully brush the pan sides with a small brush dipped in water.

4. When the syrup has reached the required temperature, remove it immediately from the heat.

Notes:
▪ *Ordinary granulated sugar is generally used for sweetmaking, but the finer the grain (i.e. caster sugar) the less chance there will be of crystallization.*

This is because the finer crystals of caster sugar dissolve more quickly than the coarser granulated sugar crystals.

▪▪ *Glucose, honey, light golden syrup, a pinch of cream of tartar or a squeeze of lemon juice may be added, which will convert some of the sugar to invert sugar, which does not crystallize so easily. If you use 4 oz. of glucose, honey or golden syrup per 1 ½ lb. sugar it will ensure that the fondant is soft and smooth, but for hard sweets (i.e. boiled sweets and toffees etc.) cream of tartar or lemon juice should be used as the glucose, honey or syrup will make them sticky.*

Sugar – Boiling Degrees

For really accurate temperature checks, a sugar thermometer should be used, but if one is not available then 'cold water tests' can be substituted. To do these tests, fill a bowl with cold water and, while the test is being carried out, remove the pan from the heat so that the temperature does not continue to rise.

The following terms are used to describe the sugar temperatures used in sweetmaking.

Thread (230°F / 110°C – 235°F / 113°C) Boil the sugar solution for 2 to 3 minutes. The syrup will spin a 2 in. thread when dropped from a fork or a spoon.

Soft ball (235°F / 113°C – 245°F / 118°C). When a drop of the syrup is put into very cold water it forms a soft ball. At 235°F the soft ball flattens on removal from the water – the higher the temperature, the firmer the ball. The soft ball stage is used for fondants and fudges.

Hard ball (245°F / 118°C – 265°F / 129°C). When dropped into cold water the syrup forms a ball which is hard enough to hold its shape, but is still pliable. The hard ball stage is used for making caramels and marshmallows.

Soft crack (270°F / 132°C – 290°F / 143°C). The syrup will separate into threads which are hard but not brittle, when dropped into the cold water. The soft crack stage is used for toffee.

Hard crack (300°F / 149°C – 310°F / 154°C). When a drop of the syrup is put into the cold water it forms threads which are both hard and brittle. Use the hard crack degree for hard toffees and rock.

Caramel (310°F / 154°C). The syrup turns a distinctive gold-brown colour and is used for pralines, etc.

EQUIPMENT

With this basic equipment it is possible to make every recipe in this book, unless special mention is made in an individual recipe.

Small fancy cutters (metal)   For cutting marshmallows, fondants etc.

Dipping forks   These can be made at home if unavailable in hardware shops. A dipping fork is a piece of firm wire about 7in long with a round or oval loop at the end to support the sweet which is to be dipped in chocolate or coating fondant.

Fondant mat   A purchased rubber mat with moulded shapes. These are sometimes difficult to purchase, but it does not prevent one from making interesting shapes with fondant which can be moulded by hand and decorated with coloured sugar strands etc.

Small sweet cases   Small decorated paper sweet cases can be purchased at most large department stores and stationers.

Colourings and flavourings   It rather depends on the brand of the colouring or flavouring as to its strength. If you are in doubt about exactly how much to use, start with just two drops and then, if a stronger colour or flavour is required, add more drop by drop.

Rubber Gloves   Used for handling hot toffee and boiled sweet mixtures.

Cornflour bed   This is a special tray for setting fondants and cream fillings and can be made quite easily at home. A wooden or tin box. 12in (30cm) square and about 3in (7½cm) deep should be filled evenly with very dry, smooth cornflour. Impressions can then be made with plaster of paris moulds glued on to a piece of wood, or alternatively with a thimble, cork or glass stopper. The candy mixture to be moulded is then poured into the impressions to a point level with the top of the cornflour and, when set, they are removed and the cornflour lightly dusted off.

Marble slab   A piece of marble, such as part of an old washstand, is ideal as a working surface for sweets. The syrups reach such high temperatures that they could damage a plastic or laminated surface. However, vitreous, porcelain or stainless steel surfaces are equally good.

Asbestos mat   Placed under saucepan to prevent caramel mixtures etc. from burning.

Sugar thermometer   A special thermometer, usually mounted on a metal scale which shows temperature and degrees of sugar boiling (see page 9). Choose a thermometer which is easy to read, with graduation from 60°F / 15°C – 360°F / 182°C   or   450°C / 232°C, preferably with a sliding clip which will fit over the side of the saucepan.

To 'season' a new thermometer, place it in cold water, bring to the boil, then leave standing in the pan until the water cools. To check the thermometer, try it (at a normal atmospheric pressure) in boiling water. The temperature of boiling water is 212°F / 100°C. If the thermometer registers higher or lower than this, make appropriate allowance when calculating the temperature of the syrup.

Always immerse the bulb of the thermometer completely in the boiling syrup. When not in use, stand the thermometer in hot water so that the temperature drops slowly. If it is plunged into cold water immediately after use in a hot syrup, the sudden fall in temperature will cause it to crack.

Heavy saucepans   Heavy saucepans made of cast iron, copper or aluminium are the most suitable for sugar boiling and sweet making. A thin saucepan will not stand the fierce heat of the boiling syrups. Use a smaller pan for smaller amounts of syrup, and a larger pan of about 4 pt (2 litre) capacity for larger amounts. Remember that the saucepans should be as deep as possible. A boiling syrup tends to rise up the sides of the pan and, if it boils over and starts to set on the cooker, it is very difficult to remove. To clean the saucepan, particularly after mak-

USEFUL COMPARATIVE ENGLISH/METRIC/AMERICAN MEASURES

Ingredient	English	Metric	American cup
Granulated sugar	8 oz	225 gm	1
Caster sugar	8 oz	225 gm	1
Brown sugar	6 oz	170 gm	1
Icing sugar	8 oz	225 gm	1 ½
Dried milk powder	8 oz	225 gm	1 ½
Currants	8 oz	225 gm	1 ½
Raisins	8 oz	225 gm	1 ½
Sultanas	8 oz	225 gm	1 ¼
Ground almonds	6 oz	170 gm	1
Cocoa powder	1 oz	30 gm	¼
Cornflour / cornstarch	1 oz	30 gm	¼
Butter	½ oz	15 gm	1 tablespoon
	4 oz	112 gm	½
Peanuts / groundnuts	4 oz	112 gm	½ +
Desiccated coconut	4 oz	112 gm	1 ½
Cake crumbs	4 oz	112 gm	1 ¼

ing toffee and caramel, fill the pan with hot water immediately, then simmer the water in the pan until all the toffee or caramel is dissolved from the sides.

Double boiler A double boiler (the top pan resting inside the bottom pan, which has boiling water in it) is particularly useful for sweet making, as the boiling water ensures even increase in temperature and also avoids the problem of the syrup sticking to the base of the pan. Syrups tend to stick in single pans which are heated on an electric plate as the element in the plate usually causes a 'hot spot' on the base of the pan.

Wooden spoons Wooden spoons should always be used to stir and scrape out pans as they do not conduct the heat of the syrup. The only time a metal spoon is more suitable is when the sugar crystals are being dissolved at the initial stage of sugar boiling. The crystals are readily visible on the shiny surface of the spoon.

Scrapers Flat bladed scrapers, such as those used by decorators, are ideal tools for moulding fondant on the working surface. The handle of the scraper should be wooden or plastic so that the heat is not conducted through the metal.

Candy hook Candy hooks are rather unusual these days, but if available they can be used for making pulled sweets. The toffee mix is pulled, folded and pulled into a thick, pliable, opaque strand which can be hooked round again with the metal sugar hook and then twisted or plaited into fancy shapes. However, with careful handling the strands can be pulled and twisted into quite interesting shapes without the aid of the hook. *Strong rubber gloves* should be worn for pulling sweets as the mixtures are usually very hot and could cause nasty burns.

Measures Accurate liquid and dry measures are essential for sweet making, as the proportion of sugar to water etc., in conjunction with the accurate gauging of the temperature, determines the kind of sweet.

Pot holders   Padded pot holders should be used for handling the saucepans, especially those with metal handles, as the amount of heat generated is quite considerable.

Palette knife   A palette knife with a flexible blade is useful for handling some sweets. The blade should be stainless.

Basin of cold water   Always keep a basin of cold water handy when making sweets based on a sugar syrup, as if any of the hot syrup or candy splashes onto the skin it can be very painful. Not only is it very hot, but the fact that it sticks to the skin means that the heat is continuous and not momentary. If an accident should occur, plunge the hands into the basin immediately.

1. Fondants

Probably the most important process in sweet making is the process of making fondant. This material (based on sugar and water) is the basis of many different candies and bonbons, chocolate creams, peppermint creams and so on.

There are two basic fondant recipes – Basic Centre Fondant and Bonbon Coating Fondant. Commercial fondants have a considerable amount of preservative incorporated in the basic mixture to give them a long shelf life, but as these preservatives are often difficult to purchase, the recipes here do not include them. This does not mean that your fondants and cream centres will not be just as delicious, but they should be eaten within a week or so of being made.

The addition of acid causes part of the sugar to turn to glucose, which gives the sweets a finer texture. Cream of tartar, acetic acid, vinegar or lemon juice can be used.

Basic Centre Fondant

The basic fondant, when made in large quantities of, say, 6 lb (3 kg) will keep for several weeks if it is in a plastic container with a tight-fitting lid. A clean damp tea towel should be packed flat onto the surface of the fondant before the lid is snapped in place. This is to prevent any crystalline formation on top of the mixture. If this does happen, when the fondant is made into individual creams, the centres will 'sugar-out' (see page 21) and become hard. This reaction occurs in the same way as a single sugar crystal remaining in the basic sugar syrup before boiling (see page 9).

Basically, a Centre Fondant is made in the following way:

The sugar and water are dissolved and brought to a temperature of 240°F / 116°C. The fondant is then worked on a marble slab until the sugar returns to the crystalline state. At this stage it will be almost rock hard, but during the next stage, kneading, it will assume a semi-liquid condition. This is the time to store it in an air-tight container to 'ripen' (see page 18). The fondant needs to ripen for at least 2 days before it is made into individual centres. The amount of fondant needed for a particular recipe is then kneaded on the marble worktop, together with any colouring or flavouring additions. These should be added *drop by drop* as they are usually very strong. Fondant which becomes too soft during this kneading process may be thickened by a teaspoon of very finely sifted icing sugar. Never add more than 1 teaspoon to an amount of fondant the size of two fists, or the sugar will cause the fondant to turn gritty and grainy.

This recipe makes approximately 1 ¼ lb (560 gm) fondant

EQUIPMENT

1 heavy based saucepan
1 metal tablespoon
1 sugar thermometer
1 spatula

INGREDIENTS

Imperial	Metric	Cup	Ingredient
¼ pt	150 ml	⅔ +	**Water**
1 lb	450 gm	2	**Granulated sugar**
1 oz	30 gm	2 tablespoons	**Glucose**
			or good pinch of
			Cream of tartar, dissolved
			in ½ teaspoon of warm water

METHOD

1. Put the water into the saucepan, add the sugar and dissolve slowly over a low heat, stirring with the metal tablespoon.

2. Bring the syrup slowly to the boil and add the glucose or cream of tartar. Boil to 240°F / 116°C and then remove from the heat. Allow to cool until the bubbles disappear from the surface.

3. Wet a marble slab or other suitable work surface (e.g. stainless steel sink top) and pour the syrup onto it. Leave it to cool to lukewarm (around 110°F / 43°C). As soon as a skin starts forming round the edges, collect the mixture together with the spatula and work it backwards and forwards using a figure-of-eight movement.

4. When the mixture becomes white and firm, knead it with the hands until the texture is even throughout.

5. The fondant is now ready to be coloured and flavoured and moulded into centres which can be left plain, dipped in chocolate (see page 151) or covered in Bonbon Coating Fondant (see below). Store as described on page 18

Note:
■ If a richer fondant is required, add a little double cream with the glucose.

Bonbon Coating Fondant

This is similar to the Basic Centre Fondant, but softer. It can also be stored in airtight, screw-top jars. Makes approximately 1 ¼ lb (560 gm) coating fondant

EQUIPMENT

1 large heavy saucepan
1 metal tablespoon
1 wooden spoon
1 sugar thermometer

INGREDIENTS

Imperial	Metric	Cup	Ingredient
1 ¼ lb	560 gm	2 ½	**Granulated sugar**
½ pt	300 cc	1 ¼	**Water**
Pinch	–	–	**Cream of tartar**

METHOD

1. Put the sugar and water into the saucepan and heat gently until the sugar has dissolv-

Right: Fondant glacé cherries, vanilla and orange bonbons, moulded fondant creams, fondant fruits and nut fondants

ed. Stir all the time with the tablespoon during the dissolving process.

2. Bring to the boil. Add the cream of tartar, dissolved in a little water, then cook to 236°F / 113°C. Remove from the heat.

3. Wipe any crystals from one side of the pan, then pour the fondant onto a marble slab or other suitable working surface and continue as for Basic Centre Fondant.

4. Store in airtight containers in the refrigerator and use as required with suitable colourings and flavourings.

Note:
■ *When the Coating Fondant is being reheated to coat Centre Fondant, it should be stirred as much as possible during the reheating and dipping process to prevent it from crusting (see page 115)*

Fondant Sugar Syrup

It is often useful to have this syrup handy when making fondants from a basic centre mixture which has been stored. If the fondant is difficult to work, add a little of the syrup. If it is too soft, add finely sifted icing sugar as described on page 15.

EQUIPMENT

1 large heavy based saucepan
1 metal tablespoon
1 sugar thermometer
1 metal sieve lined with muslin

INGREDIENTS

Imperial	Metric	Cup	Ingredient
1 lb	450 gm	2	**Granulated sugar**
½ pt	300 ml	1 ¼	**Water**

METHOD

1. Put the sugar and water into the pan and heat slowly, stirring with the metal spoon until the sugar has dissolved.

2. Bring the syrup to the boil and continue to boil until the mixture forms a thick syrup texture (216°F / 102°C).

3. Strain carefully through the muslin. Store in screw-topped bottles. This syrup will keep for a month or more.

■ *See page 168 for recipes for uncooked fondants.*

Fondant Creams

1. Follow recipe and method for Basic Centre Fondant and add a little double cream, if available, to improve the texture and flavour.

2. Divide the mixture into portions and flavour and colour as desired with coffee essence, rum essence, fruit oils, rosewater, etc. (see suggested flavourings below).

3. Roll the fondant out to a thickness of about ½ in / 1 ¼ cm and then cut into fancy shapes with metal cutters or mould by hand. If a fondant mat (see page 10) is available, melt the fondant in a basin over hot water, add a little of the fondant sugar syrup and then pour into the rubber moulds, using a small funnel or teaspoon.

4. Leave the shapes to harden. For a more professional finish, dip or coat with chocolate (see page 151) and then roll in chopped nuts, desiccated coconut or chocolate vermicelli, alternatively in Bonbon Coating Fondant (see page 16).

■ *Uncoated fondants are traditionally displayed in plain fluted sweet cases. They should be allowed to harden for about 4 hours before being put into the paper cases.*

Flavouring Fondant Creams

Fondant lends itself particularly well to a whole variety of colourings and flavourings. Normal food colours, which can be bought at most good chemists or department stores, are suitable for colouring, and if available, fruit oils or essences (e.g. oil of orange, oil of lemon) should be used to flavour the sweets as so little is required to give a good flavour that the fondant does not become too soft. However, if it is difficult to obtain these oils and essences, finely grated orange peel, or finely grated lemon peel can be substituted quite satisfactorily.

The amount of flavouring and colouring depends entirely on the amount of Basic Centre Fondant used – the most accurate guide is to add a few drops, then taste, then add more if required. These flavourings and colourings are generally very strong and should be used sparingly.

Fruit or Nut Fondant

1. Follow recipe and method for Fondant Creams.
2. Add 4 oz (112 gm / 1 cup) chopped unsalted nuts (not peanuts) or sultanas, currants or raisins to each 1 lb (450 gm) of fondant made.

Neapolitan Fondant Creams

1. Follow recipe and method for Basic Centre Fondant.
2. Divide the batch of fondant into three parts. Leave one part white and flavour it. Then colour and flavour the other two parts differently.
3. Roll each part into a thin roll, place one on top of the other, then roll out to the thickness of a finger.
4. Cut into slices and allow to become firm on a sheet of greaseproof paper. Decorate with silver balls or small crystallized flowers.

Fondant Fruits

Fruits such as glacé cherries, crystallized ginger, glacé pineapple, tiny bunches of grapes, etc., can quite successfully be dipped in plain or coloured fondant.

1. Follow recipe and method for Basic Centre Fondant.
2. Place in a basin over hot water and melt until the mixture coats the back of a wooden spoon easily but not too thickly. Use a little sugar syrup if necessary.
3. Using a skewer or dipping fork (see page 110), dip the fruits into the fondant and then put them onto greaseproof paper to set. Only use small quantities of fondant at a time. If too much is used it will overheat and become dull in the basin.

Note:

■ *Fondant can also be used for filling such fruits as apricot halves, pitted prunes, pitted dates, etc. Fill the fruits with spoonfuls of Basic Centre Fondant, coloured if desired, and flavoured with a few chopped nuts. Roll the filled fruits in granulated sugar and allow to set.*

Vanilla and Walnut Fondant Creams

1. Follow recipe and method for Basic Centre Fondant to make 1 lb (450 gm) of fondant.
2. Flavour with a few drops of vanilla essence and knead in 4 oz (112 gm / 1 cup) chopped walnuts.
3. Shape as Fondant Creams.

Orange and Almond Fondant Creams

1. Follow recipe and method for Basic Centre Fondant to make 1 lb (450 gm) fondant.
2. Flavour with a few drops of oil of orange or add 1 dessertspoon of finely grated orange peel, and 4 oz (112 gm / 1 cup) chopped toasted almonds.
3. Shape as Fondant Creams.

Lemon and Toasted Coconut Fondant Creams

1. Follow recipe and method for Basic Centre Fondant to make 1 lb (450 gm) of fondant.
2. Flavour with a few drops of oil of lemon or 1 dessertspoon of finely grated lemon peel and 4 oz (112 gm / 1½ cups) of toasted desiccated coconut.
3. Shape as Fondant Creams.

Rum and Raisin Fondant Creams

1. Follow recipe and method for Basic Centre Fondant to make 1 lb (450 gm) fondant.
2. Flavour with a few drops of rum essence and add 4 oz (112 gm / ¾ cup) of chopped raisins.
3. Shape as Fondant Creams.

Peppermint Fondant Creams

1. Follow recipe and method for Basic Centre Fondant to make 1 lb (450 gm) fondant.
2. Flavour with a few drops of oil of peppermint and either leave white or colour pale green with a few drops of green colouring.
3. Peppermint creams are traditionally flat and round in shape, so roll out and cut with a plain round cutter.

Maraschino Fondant Creams

1. Follow recipe and method for Basic Centre Fondant to make 1 lb (450 gm) fondant.
2. Colour with a few drops of pink colouring and add 4 tablespoons chopped maraschino cherries.
3. Roll into round balls about the size of a large cherry and then leave to set on waxed paper.

Pistachio Fondant Creams

1. Follow recipe and method for Basic Centre Fondant to make 1 lb (450 gm) fondant.
2. Colour with a little green colouring and add 4 tablespoons of chopped pistachio nuts.
3. Shape into small oval shapes a little bigger than an almond, then leave to set on waxed paper.

BONBONS

Bonbons are very popular on the Continent, especially in Belgium. Essentially they are pieces of flavoured Centre Fondant which are dipped in Coating Fondant and decorated with silver balls, crystallized flowers, etc.

The centres should be rolled into round marble sized balls and left on waxed paper until

---

Left: Moulded and shaped fondants, peppermint creams, pistachio and lemon creams, and Neopolitan creams

the tops have a light crust on them. When the crust has formed, turn them upside down so that the bottom gets a light crust as well. This is important as if they are still very soft when dipped, this will spoil not only the Coating Fondant but the centre as well.

Dipping Bonbons

1. Have ready a clean sheet of waxed paper near the pan to put the dipped centres on. Put the Coating Fondant into a basin over a pan of hot water, or into the top half of a double boiler (see page 11).
2. Heat to just below boiling point and keep it at that temperature, stirring frequently to prevent a crust from forming.
3. Bonbons cannot be dipped by hand, so a dipping fork must be used. Place the prepared centre onto the centre of the loop of the fork and lower into the melted fondant, turning it over immediately to cover it completely with the coating. The top of the centre will then be positioned downwards in the fondant. Put the loop of the fork underneath the fondant centre, lift it out, tap the fork on the edge of the pan to remove any excess coating and then draw it across the edge of the pan, taking care not to scrape the top of the bonbon itself on the pan.
4. Carry the bonbon over to the waxed paper and invert the fork so that the bonbon is turned onto its base on the waxed paper. Leave the fork on top of the fondant for a minute, then with one lift, straight up, remove the fork so that the Coating Fondant is pulled into a traditional 'crown' shape.
5. Decorate with silver balls or small crystallized flowers. These must be placed on the top of the bonbon immediately after the 'crown' has been made with the dipping fork. Store in a cool place and handle only by the paper sweet cases as the surface will be marked quite easily by warm fingers. Allow the bonbons to stand for an hour or two so that the coating is set completely on the base of the sweets.

Note:
■ Bonbons are traditionally displayed in simple white paper sweet cases and should be removed from the waxed paper with a peeling motion which avoids pulling the base away from the top.

Vanilla Bonbons

1. Follow recipe and method for Basic Centre Fondant.

2. Flavour with a few drops of vanilla essence.
3. Mould the fondant into small balls and allow to dry out on waxed paper (see method above).
4. Follow recipe for Basic Coating Fondant.
5. Flavour with a few drops of vanilla essence.
6. Dip centres in coating (see method above).

Vanilla Walnut Bonbons

1. Follow recipe and method for Vanilla Walnut Creams.
2. Follow recipe and method for Basic Coating Fondant.
3. Add a few drops of vanilla essence.
4. Dip centres in coating (see method above).

Orange Bonbons

1. Follow recipe and method for Orange and Almond Fondant Creams.
2. Follow recipe and method for Basic Coating Fondant.
3. Colour with a little orange colouring.
4. Dip centres in coating (see method above).

Maraschino Bonbons

1. Follow recipe and method for Maraschino Fondant Creams.
2. Follow recipe and method for Basic Coating Fondant.
3. Colour with a little pink colouring.
4. Dip centres in coating (see method above).

Pistachio Bonbons

1. Follow recipe and method for Pistachio Fondant Creams.
2. Follow recipe for Basic Coating Fondant.
3. Colour with a little green colouring.
4. Dip centres in coating (see method above).

Coffee Bonbons

1. Follow recipe and method for Basic Centre Fondant.
2. Flavour with a few drops of coffee essence and allow to dry out on waxed paper (see method above).
3. Follow recipe and method for Basic Coating Fondant.
4. Flavour with a few drops of vanilla essence.
5. Dip centres in coating (see method above).

2. Fudges

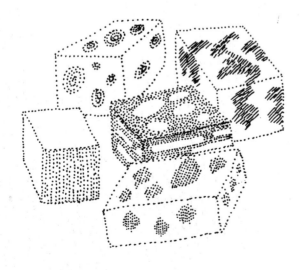

Fudges are made by boiling the sugar syrup to the soft ball stage (240°F / 116°C) (see page 9.). The cooked syrup is then cooled and stirred or beaten until it is *almost* firm.

To shape fudge, it should be turned into a shallow buttered tin, square or oblong in shape, or onto a lightly greased marble slab, and then marked into squares.

Good fudge should be smooth, creamy and soft in texture with a rich middle brown colour and a glossy top surface. There are endless varieties of flavourings and additions which can be made to the basic fudge recipe, and they can also be dipped in chocolate for an extra special finish (see page 151).

Vanilla Fudge (method 1)

Makes approximately 1 lb (450 gm) fudge

EQUIPMENT

1 large heavy based saucepan
1 metal tablespoon
1 sugar thermometer
1 wooden spoon
1 lightly greased shallow tin 8 in x 6 in (20 cm x 15 cm)
1 sharp knife

Below: The utensils needed in the preparing and cutting of fudge

INGREDIENTS

Imperial	Metric	Cup	Ingredients
1 lb	450 gm	2	**Granulated sugar**
2 oz	56 gm	¼	**Butter**
¼ pt	150 ml	⅔	**Evaporated milk**
¼ pt	150 ml	⅔	**Fresh milk**
3 drops	–	–	**Vanilla essence**

METHOD

1. Put the sugar, butter and two sorts of milk into the saucepan and heat very gently, stirring with the tablespoon until all the sugar has dissolved and the fat has melted. Bring the mixture to the boil and boil steadily until the thermometer registers 240°F / 116°C. Stir the mixture occasionally.

2. Remove the pan from the heat and place on a cold surface (e.g. stainless steel sink top).

3. Add the vanilla essence and beat the mixture with the wooden spoon until it becomes thick and creamy and 'grains' (see page 192).

4. Pour the fudge into the greased tin immediately, otherwise it will begin to set in the pan. Leave until nearly cold.

5. Mark the cooled fudge into squares with the sharp knife. When it is completely cold and firm, cut into squares.

Note:
■ Fudge can be stored quite successfully in an airtight tin, but if you want to include fudge squares in a box of assorted sweets, wrap them in plain squares of thin waxed paper.

Cherry Mallow Fudge

1. Follow recipe and method for Vanilla Fudge (1).

2. Add 2 oz (56 gm / ½ cup) chopped glacé cherries and 4 oz (112 gm / 1½ cup) chopped marshmallows to the fudge just before the temperature reaches 240°F / 116°C.

3. Finish as for Vanilla Fudge.

Nut Mallow Fudge

1. Follow recipe and method for Vanilla Fudge (1).

2. Add 2 oz (56 gm / ½ cup) chopped walnuts and 4 oz (112 gm / 1½ cup) chopped marshmallows just before the temperature reaches 240°F / 116°C.

3. Finish as for Vanilla Fudge.

Ginger Fudge

1. Follow recipe and method for Vanilla Fudge (1).

2. Add 4 tablespoons chopped crystallized ginger just before the temperature reaches 240°F / 116°C.

3. Finish as for Vanilla Fudge.

Tangy Fruit Fudge

1. Follow recipe for Vanilla Fudge (1).

2. Add 4 tablespoons chopped mixed peel just before the temperature reaches 240°F / 116°C.

3. Finish as for Vanilla Fudge.

Coconut Fudge

1. Follow recipe and method for Vanilla Fudge (1).

2. Add 4 tablespoons desiccated coconut to the fudge just before the temperature reaches 240°F / 116°C.

3. Finish as for Vanilla Fudge.

Cinnamon Fudge

1. Follow recipe and method for Vanilla Fudge (1).
2. Add 2 teaspoons powdered cinnamon to the fudge just before the temperature reaches 240°F / 116°C.
3. Finish as for Vanilla Fudge.

Pineapple Fudge

1. Follow the recipe for Vanilla Fudge (1).
2. Add 4 tablespoons chopped glacé pineapple, or 4 tablespoons well drained canned pineapple, chopped in pieces, just before the temperature reaches 240°F / 116°C.
3. Finish as for Vanilla Fudge.

Apricot Fudge

1. Soak 4 oz (112 gm) dried apricots overnight in water until they plump and swell up, then chop them.

2. Add to the recipe for Vanilla Fudge (1) just before the temperature reaches 240°F / 116°C.
3. Finish as for Vanilla Fudge.

Date Fudge

1. Follow the recipe and method for Vanilla Fudge (1).
2. Add 4 tablespoons chopped dates just before the temperature reaches 240°F / 116°C.
3. Finish as for Vanilla Fudge.

Peppermint Fudge

1. Follow recipe and method for Vanilla Fudge (1).
2. Add ½ teaspoon peppermint essence or oil of peppermint to the fudge just before the temperature reaches 240°F / 116°C.
3. Finish as for Vanilla Fudge.

Vanilla Fudge (method 2)

Makes approximately 1 lb (450 gm) fudge

EQUIPMENT

1 large heavy based saucepan
1 metal tablespoon
1 wooden spoon
1 lightly greased shallow tin 8 in x 6 in (20 cm x 15 cm)
1 sharp knife

INGREDIENTS

Imperial	Metric	Cup	Ingredient
1 lb	*450 gm*	*2*	**Granulated sugar**
3 tablespoons	*–*	*–*	**Water**
2 oz	*56 gm*	*¼*	**Butter**
2 tablespoons	*–*	*–*	**Golden syrup**
¾ pt	*450 ml*	*2*	**Sweetened condensed milk**
3 drops	*–*	*–*	**Vanilla essence**

METHOD

1. Put the sugar and the water into the saucepan and cook over a very low heat. Stir with the metal tablespoon so that you can see when the sugar crystals have completely dissolved.
2. Add the butter and the syrup and stir

very gently with the metal spoon until the butter has melted.

3. Pour in the condensed milk, raise the heat and stir with the wooden spoon until the mixture comes to the boil. Boil rapidly, stirring all the time, for 20 - 25 minutes.

4. Remove the pan from the cooker and place on a cold surface.

5. Add the vanilla essence and beat with the wooden spoon until the mixture thickens.

6. Pour the fudge quickly into the greased tin and leave it to cool. Mark into squares as Vanilla Fudge (1) and cut out when completely cold. Wrap as Vanilla Fudge (1).

Creamy Chocolate Fudge

Makes approximately 1 ½ lb (675 gm) fudge

EQUIPMENT

1 large heavy based saucepan
1 wooden spoon
1 lightly greased shallow tin, 8 in x 6 in
(20 cm x 15 cm)
1 sharp knife

Above: Vanilla and chocolate vanilla fudge, cherry mallows

Left: Creamy chocolate and fruit and nut fudge, four-minute fudge, and five-minute crunchy peanut fudge

INGREDIENTS

Imperial	Metric	Cup	Ingredient
¾ pt	450 ml	2	*Sweetened condensed milk*
1 lb	450 gm	2	*Granulated sugar*
3 tablespoons	–	–	*Clear honey*
4 oz	112 gm	½	*Butter*
1 teaspoon	–	–	*Vanilla essence*
4 oz	112 gm	–	*Grated plain chocolate*

METHOD

1. Put the condensed milk, sugar, honey and butter into the saucepan, bring to the boil as quickly as possible and allow to boil fast, without boiling over, for exactly 10 minutes. Stir the mixture with the wooden spoon all the time.

2. Remove the pan from the heat, then stir in the vanilla essence and grated chocolate and beat for 5 minutes until the mixture is thick.

3. Pour quickly into the greased tin and mark into squares when almost cold. When completely cold and firm, cut into squares. Store in an airtight tin or wrap in thin waxed paper.

Marshmallow Chocolate Fudge

1. Follow recipe and method for Creamy Chocolate Fudge.

2. Just before beating add 16 chopped marshmallows to the fudge.

3. Complete as for Creamy Chocolate Fudge.

Fruit and Nut Chocolate Fudge

1. Follow recipe and method for Creamy Chocolate Fudge.

2. Just before beating add 2 oz (56 gm / ½ cup) chopped nuts and 2 oz. (56 gm / ½ cup) seedless raisins.

3. Complete as for Creamy Chocolate Fudge.

Coffee Walnut Fudge

1. Follow recipe and method for Creamy Chocolate Fudge but omit chocolate and vanilla.

2. Add 1½ level tablespoons instant coffee blended with 1 tablespoon of water. Add this with the condensed milk.

3. Stir in 2 oz (56 gm / ½ cup) chopped walnuts before beating away from the heat.

4. Complete as for Creamy Chocolate Fudge.

Five-Minute Peanut Fudge

Makes approximately 12 oz (340 gm) fudge

EQUIPMENT

1 heavy based saucepan
1 pudding basin to fit inside the saucepan
1 wooden spoon
1 lightly greased shallow tin, 6 in (15 cm) square
1 sharp knife

30

INGREDIENTS

Imperial	Metric	Cup	Ingredient
¼ pt	150 ml	⅔	*Sweetened condensed milk*
2 tablespoons	–	–	*Smooth peanut butter*
4 drops	–	–	*Vanilla essence*
½ lb	225 gm	1 ½	*Icing sugar*

METHOD

1. Put the condensed milk and peanut butter into the pudding basin and mix well with the wooden spoon.
2. Stand the basin in a pan of boiling water so that the water comes about halfway up the sides of the basin. Cook for about 5 minutes, stirring all the time. Remove from the heat.
3. Add the vanilla essence and the icing sugar, then turn the fudge into the greased tin and place in the refrigerator. Cut when cold. Wrap as for Vanilla Fudge (1).

Crunchy Five-minute Peanut Fudge

1. Follow recipe and method for Five-Minute Peanut Fudge.
2. Use crunchy peanut butter instead of smooth peanut butter.

Rum Cream Fudge

Makes approximately 1 ½ lb (675 gm) fudge

EQUIPMENT

1 large heavy based saucepan
1 metal tablespoon
1 sugar thermometer
1 wooden spoon
1 lightly greased shallow tin, 8 in x 6 in (20 cm x 15 cm)
1 sharp knife

INGREDIENTS

Imperial	Metric	Cup	Ingredient
1 ½ lb	675 gm	3	*Granulated sugar*
8 fl oz	240 ml	1	*Single cream*
1 pinch	–	–	*Cream of tartar*
½ teaspoon	–	–	*Vanilla essence*
1 tablespoon	–	–	*Rum*

METHOD

1. Put the sugar and cream into the saucepan and heat very gently until the sugar dissolves. Stir the mixture with the tablespoon while the sugar is dissolving.
2. Bring to the boil and add the cream of tartar, dissolved in 1 teaspoon of water. Boil until the thermometer registers 240°F / 116°C.

Above: Penuche and nutty penuche, fruit and banana fudge

---

3. Remove from the heat and allow to cool. Add the vanilla essence and rum.
4. Beat the fudge until it becomes thick and creamy and starts to 'grain' (see page192), then pour it quickly into the prepared tin.
5. Mark it into squares when it is almost cool. When completely set, cut with a sharp knife. Wrap as for Vanilla Fudge (1).

Brandy Cream Fudge

1. Follow recipe and method for Rum Cream Fudge.
2. Add 1 tablespoon brandy instead of the rum.

Gaelic Cream Fudge

1. Follow recipe and method for Rum Cream Fudge.

2. Use 1 tablespoon Irish whiskey instead of the rum, together with 1 tablespoon coffee essence.

Crème de Menthe Cream Fudge

1. Follow recipe and method for Rum Cream Fudge.
2. Add 1 tablespoon Crème de Menthe instead of the rum.

Cointreau Cream Fudge

1. Follow recipe and method for Rum Cream Fudge.
2. Add 1 tablespoon Cointreau instead of the rum.

Chartreuse Cream Fudge

1. Follow recipe and method for Rum Cream Fudge.
2. Add 1 tablespoon Chartreuse instead of the rum.

Peppermint Cream Fudge

1.   Follow recipe and method for Rum Cream Fudge.
2.   Add 1 teaspoon of peppermint essence instead of the rum.

Almond Cream Fudge

1.   Follow recipe and method for Rum Cream Fudge.
2.   Omit the rum and add 4 tablespoons chopped roasted almonds just before beating the fudge.

Coconut Cream Fudge

1.   Follow recipe and method for Rum Cream Fudge·

2.   Omit the rum and add 4 tablespoons toasted coconut just before beating the fudge.

Hazelnut Cream Fudge

1.   Follow recipe and method for Rum Cream Fudge.
2.   Omit the rum and add 4 tablespoons chopped toasted hazelnuts just before beating the fudge.

Brazil Nut Cream Fudge

1.   Follow recipe and method for Rum Cream Fudge
2.   Omit the rum and add 4 tablespoons chopped brazil nuts just before beating the fudge.

Penuche (Rich brown fudge)

Makes approximately 2 lb (900 gm) fudge

EQUIPMENT

1 large heavy based saucepan
1 metal tablespoon
1 wooden spoon
1 sugar thermometer
1 lightly greased shallow tin, 7 in (18 cm) square
1 sharp knife

INGREDIENTS

Imperial	Metric	Cup	Ingredient
1 lb	*450 gm*	*3*	**Light soft brown sugar**
6 fl oz	*180 ml*	*¾*	**Fresh milk**
1 tablespoon	*–*	*–*	**Margarine**
1 tablespoon	*–*	*–*	**Golden syrup**
4 drops	*–*	*–*	**Vanilla essence**

METHOD

1.   Put the sugar, milk, margarine and syrup into the saucepan. Heat gently, stirring all the time with the metal tablespoon, until the sugar dissolves.
2.   Bring the mixture to the boil, then cook steadily until the temperature is 240°F / 116°C. The fudge should be stirred occasionally while it is boiling
3.   Remove from the heat and cool until the fudge is lukewarm.

4.   Add the vanilla essence and beat with the wooden spoon until it is thick and creamy and starts to grain' (see page 192.). Quickly pour the fudge into the greased tin and cut into squares when cold. Wrap as for Vanilla Fudge (1).

Nutty Penuche

1. Follow recipe and method for Penuche.
2. After beating the fudge, stir in 2 oz (56 gm / ½ cup) chopped walnuts, hazelnuts or almonds.

Raisin Penuche

1. Follow recipe and method for Penuche.
2. Add 2 oz (56 gm / ½ cup) seedless raisins after beating the fudge.

Cherry Penuche

1. Follow recipe and method for Penuche.

2. Add 2 oz (5·6 gm / ½ cup) chopped glacé cherries after beating the fudge.

Pineapple Penuche

1. Follow the recipe for Penuche.
2. Add 2 oz (56 gm / ½ cup) chopped glacé pineapple after beating the fudge.

Ginger Penuche

1. Follow the recipe for Penuche.
2. Add 2 oz (56 gm / ½ cup) chopped stem ginger after beating the fudge.

Fruit Fudge

Makes approximately 2 ½ lb (1,125 gm) fudge

EQUIPMENT

1 large heavy based saucepan
1 metal tablespoon
1 wooden spoon
1 sugar thermometer
1 lightly greased shallow tin, 12 in x 4 in (30 cm x 10 cm)
1 sharp knife

INGREDIENTS

Imperial	Metric	Cup	Ingredient
2 lb	900 gm	4	**Granulated sugar**
½ pt	300 ml	1 ¼	**Evaporated milk**
4 oz	112 gm	½	**Butter**
½	–	–	**Large orange, grated rind**
4 tablespoons	–	–	**Orange juice**

METHOD

1. Put the sugar, milk and butter into the saucepan and heat slowly until the sugar has dissolved, stirring all the time with the table-spoon.
2. Add the grated orange rind and the orange juice, bring the mixture to the boil and cook steadily until the temperature reaches 240°F / 116°C. Stir during the boiling period to prevent the fudge from sticking to the base of the pan.
3. As soon as the temperature is reached, remove the pan from the heat and place on a cool surface. Beat with the wooden spoon until thick and creamy and beginning to 'grain' (see page 192)
4. Pour immediately into the prepared tin. Mark into squares when cool and cut with a sharp knife when completely cold. Pack as for Vanilla Fudge (1).

Left: Caramel fudge, fudge layers, tutti-frutti fudge

Apricot Fudge

1.   Follow recipe and method for Fruit Fudge, omitting the orange peel and orange juice.
2.   Add 4 tablespoons chopped, drained, canned apricots after beating the fudge.

Lemon Fudge

1.   Follow the recipe and method for Fruit Fudge.

2.   Add the grated rind of ½ a lemon and 4 tablespoons of lemon juice instead of orange rind and juice.

Pineapple Fudge

1.   Follow the recipe for Fruit Fudge but omit the orange peel and the orange juice.
2.   Stir in 4 tablespoons chopped, drained canned pineapple after beating the fudge.

Caramel Fudgies

Makes approximately 1 ¾ lb (780 gm) fudge

EQUIPMENT

1 large heavy frying pan
1 large heavy saucepan
1 wooden spoon
1 sugar thermometer
1 lightly greased tin, 8 in (20 cm) square

INGREDIENTS

Imperial	Metric	Cup	Ingredient
1 ½ lb	*675 gm*	*3*	**Granulated sugar**
8 fl oz	*240 ml*	*1*	**Top of the milk or single cream**
Pinch	*–*	*–*	**Baking powder**
1 tablespoon	*–*	*–*	**Butter**
½ teaspoon	*–*	*–*	**Vanilla essence**
4 oz	*112 gm*	*1*	**Chopped walnuts**

METHOD

1.   Put 8 oz (225 gm / 1 cup) of the granulated sugar into the frying pan and melt over a very low heat until the sugar starts to turn golden brown and becomes liquid.
2.   Put the remaining 1 lb (450 gm / 2 cups) granulated sugar and the top of the milk or single cream into the heavy saucepan and bring to a gentle boil, stirring continuously.
3.   As soon as the sugar and milk mixture is really boiling, pour in the caramelized sugar from the frying pan.
4.   Continue boiling, stirring constantly until the temperature reaches 238°F / 114°C. Remove from the heat.
5.   Stir in the baking powder so that the mixture foams really well, then add the butter, this time without stirring.
6.   Cool the fudge to 110°F / 43°C, then add the vanilla essence and beat well until the fudge starts to 'grain' (see page 192).
7.   Stir in the chopped nuts and then turn into the prepared tin, cool until firm and cut into 1 in (2 ½ cm) squares. Wrap in lightly waxed paper.

Caramel Orange Fudgies

1.   Follow recipe and method for Caramel Fudgies.

2.   Add the finely grated peel of 1 large sweet orange with the butter.
3.   Continue as for Caramel Fudgies.

Ginger Caramel Fudgies

1. Follow recipe and method for Caramel Fudgies, omitting the vanilla essence.
2. Add 4 tablespoons chopped stem ginger with the chopped nuts.
3. Finish as for Caramel Fudgies.

Almond Caramel Fudgies

1. Follow recipe and method for Caramel Fudgies.
2. Substitute chopped toasted almonds for the chopped walnuts.
3. Finish as for Caramel Fudgies.

Pineapple Caramel Fudgies

1. Follow recipe and method for Caramel Fudgies, omitting the vanilla essence.
2. Add 4 tablespoons chopped crystallized or canned pineapple with the chopped walnuts.
3. Finish as for Caramel Fudgies.

Apricot Caramel Fudgies

1. Follow recipe and method for Caramel Fudgies.
2. Add 4 tablespoons chopped canned apricots with the chopped walnuts.
3. Finish as for Caramel Fudgies.

Hazelnut Caramel Fudgies

1. Follow recipe and method for Caramel Fudgies.

2. Substitute chopped toasted hazelnuts for the chopped walnuts.
3. Finish as for Caramel Fudgies.

Brazil Nut Caramel Fudgies

1. Follow recipe and method for Caramel Fudgies.
2. Substitute chopped brazil nuts for the chopped walnuts.
3. Finish as for Caramel Fudgies.

Coconut Caramel Fudgies

1. Follow recipe and method for Caramel Fudgies.
2. Substitute 4 tablespoons desiccated coconut for the chopped walnuts.
3. Finish as for Caramel Fudgies.

Lemon Caramel Fudgies

1. Follow recipe and method for Caramel Fudgies.
2. Add ½ teaspoon lemon essence instead of the vanilla essence.
3. Finish as for Caramel Fudgies.

Raisin Caramel Fudgies

1. Follow recipe and method for Caramel Fudgies.
2. Add 4 tablespoons seedless raisins.
3. Finish as for Caramel Fudgies.

Walnut Buttermilk Fudge

Makes approximately 1 ½ lb (675 gm) fudge

EQUIPMENT

1 large heavy saucepan
1 metal tablespoon
1 wooden spoon
1 sugar thermometer
1 lightly greased tin, 8 in (20 cm) square

INGREDIENTS

Imperial	Metric	Cup	Ingredient
8 fl oz	240 ml	1	**Buttermilk**
1 level teaspoon	–	–	**Baking powder**
2 tablespoons	–	–	**Clear honey**
1 lb	450 gm	2	**Granulated sugar**
1 oz	30 gm	2 tablespoons	**Butter**
4 oz	112 gm	1	**Chopped walnuts**

METHOD

1. Put the buttermilk and the baking powder into the saucepan and allow it to stand for about 20 minutes so that the baking powder dissolves.

2. Add the clear honey and the sugar to the buttermilk in the saucepan, then heat over a low heat, stirring continuously, with the tablespoon until all the sugar has dissolved.

3. Bring the fudge mixture to the boil, and cook until the temperature reaches 238°F / 114°C, stirring occasionally to prevent the fudge from sticking to the pan.

4. Remove the pan from the heat, add the butter without stirring and cool to 110°F / 43°C, then beat until the fudge starts to 'grain' (see page 192). Stir in walnuts and turn into the prepared tin.

5. As soon as the fudge has cooled a little, mark into 1 in (2½ cm) squares, then when it is completely cold, remove from the tin and cut into pieces. Wrap in lightly waxed paper.

Note:
■ *As buttermilk is often difficult to obtain, you could use sour milk as a substitute.*

Almond Buttermilk Fudge

1. Follow recipe and method for Walnut Buttermilk Fudge.
2. Substitute chopped blanched almonds for the chopped walnuts.
3. Finish as for Walnut Buttermilk Fudge.

Brazil Nut Buttermilk Fudge

1. Follow recipe and method for Walnut Buttermilk Fudge.
2. Substitute chopped brazil nuts for the chopped walnuts.
3. Finish as for Walnut Buttermilk Fudge.

Coconut Buttermilk Fudge

1. Follow recipe and method for Walnut Buttermilk Fudge.
2. Substitute desiccated coconut for the chopped walnuts.
3. Finish as for Walnut Buttermilk Fudge.

Hazelnut Buttermilk Fudge

1. Follow recipe and method for Walnut Buttermilk Fudge.

2. Substitute chopped hazelnuts for the chopped walnuts.
3. Finish as for Walnut Buttermilk Fudge.

Raisin Buttermilk Fudge

1. Follow recipe and method for Walnut Buttermilk Fudge.
2. Substitute seedless raisins for the chopped walnuts.
3. Finish as for Walnut Buttermilk Fudge.

Right: Polkadot peanut fudge, nutty fudge squares, soft peanut fudge and West Country honey fudge

Mocha Fudge Supreme

Makes approximately 2 lb (900 gm) fudge

EQUIPMENT

1 large heavy saucepan
1 metal tablespoon
1 wooden spoon
1 sugar thermometer
1 lightly greased tin, 8 in (20 cm) square
1 double boiler, or a small pudding basin standing in a pan of hot water
1 sharp knife

INGREDIENTS

Imperial	Metric	Cup	Ingredient
6 fl oz	180 ml	¾	**Milk**
4 fl oz	120 ml	½	**Single cream**
Pinch	–	–	**Salt**
1 ½ lb	675 gm	3	**Granulated sugar**
2 tablespoons	–	–	**Instant coffee granules**
1 tablespoon	–	–	**Golden syrup**
2 oz	56 gm	¼	**Butter**
1 teaspoon	–	–	**Vanilla essence**
6 oz	170 gm	6 oz	**Plain chocolate**
2 oz	56 gm	½	**Roasted almonds**

METHOD

1.   Put the milk, single cream, salt, sugar, coffee granules and golden syrup into the saucepan and heat very gently, stirring all the time with the tablespoon until the sugar crystals have completely dissolved.

2.   Bring the mixture to the boil and boil gently, without stirring, until the temperature reaches 238°F / 114°C. Remove from the heat.

3.   Add the butter and vanilla essence but do not stir at this stage. Cool the fudge without disturbing it to 110°F / 43°C.

4.   Beat the fudge with a wooden spoon until it starts to thicken and 'grain' (see page 192) then turn into the prepared tin.

5.   Meanwhile, break the chocolate into pieces and either place in the top of the double boiler or into a small basin over a pan of hot water.

6.   When it has melted spread it evenly over the cooled fudge, then chop the roasted almonds and sprinkle them over the top.

7.   When the chocolate has set, cut the fudge into small 1 in (2 ½ cm) squares or narrow bars and store in an airtight tin.

Note:
■ This type of fudge is not really suitable for long-term storage or for sending through the post, as the chocolate will become soft and sticky.

Banana Fudge

Makes approximately 1 lb (450 gm) fudge

EQUIPMENT

1 large heavy saucepan

1 metal tablespoon
1 wooden spoon
1 sugar thermometer
2 lb loaf tin, lightly greased
1 large sharp knife

INGREDIENTS

Imperial	Metric	Cup	Ingredients
12 oz	*340 gm*	*1 ½*	**Granulated sugar**
9 oz	*250 gm*	*1 ½*	**Soft brown sugar**
4 oz	*112 gm*		**Dessert chocolate (broken into pieces)**
6 fl oz	*180 ml*	*¾*	**Milk (full cream)**
1	*–*	*–*	**Mashed banana (not too ripe)**
Pinch	*–*	*–*	**Salt**
2 tablespoons	*–*	*–*	**Golden syrup**
3 oz	*80 gm*	*⅓*	**Margarine**
4 drops	*–*	*–*	**Vanilla essence**

METHOD

1. Put both types of sugar, pieces of chocolate, milk, banana, salt and syrup into the saucepan and heat gently, stirring all the time, until the sugar crystals have completely dissolved.

2. Raise the heat a little and allow the fudge to boil gently, stirring occasionally to prevent sticking, until the temperature reaches 240°F / 116°C. Remove from the heat.

3. Add the margarine but do not stir at this stage. Allow the fudge to cool to 110° F / 43°C, then add the vanilla essence and beat with a wooden spoon until the fudge begins to 'grain' (see page 192).

4. Turn immediately into the prepared loaf tin and mark into about 20 pieces while the fudge is still a little warm. Allow to cool and set completely, then cut and wrap in lightly waxed paper.

Banana Walnut Fudge

1. Follow recipe and method for Banana Fudge.

2. Immediately after turning the cooked fudge into the loaf tin, press 2 oz (56 gm / ½ cup) finely chopped walnuts into the top of the warm fudge.

3. Mark, cool and cut as for Banana Fudge

Banana Hazelnut Fudge

1. Follow recipe and method for Banana Fudge.

2. Add 4 tablespoons chopped roasted hazelnuts with the vanilla essence.

3. Finish as for Banana Fudge.

Banana Coconut Fudge

1. Follow recipe and method for Banana Fudge.

2. Add 4 tablespoons toasted desiccated coconut with the vanilla essence.

3. Finish as for Banana Fudge.

Polka Dot Peanut Fudge

Makes approx 1 lb (450 gm) fudge

EQUIPMENT

1 large heavy saucepan
1 metal tablespoon
1 wooden spoon
1 sugar thermometer
1 lb loaf tin, lightly greased
1 large sharp knife

INGREDIENTS

Imperial	Metric	Cup	Ingredient
5 fl oz	150 ml	⅔	**Milk (full cream)**
1 lb	450 gm	2	**Granulated sugar**
1 oz	30 gm	2 tablespoons	**Margarine**
3 tablespoons	–	–	**Crunchy peanut butter**
1 teaspoon	–	–	**Vanilla essence**
3 oz	80 gm	½	**Chocolate 'polka dots'**

METHOD

1. Put the milk and sugar into the saucepan and heat very gently, stirring all the time with the tablespoon to speed the dissolving of the sugar.

2. When the sugar crystals have completely dissolved, bring to the boil, then continue to boil slowly, stirring continuously, until the temperature reaches 238°F / 114°C. Remove from the heat.

3. Add the margarine to the sugar mixture. Do not stir at this stage but allow to cool to 110°F / 43°C.

4. Add the peanut butter and vanilla essence and then beat the mixture with a wooden spoon until the fudge starts to 'grain' (see page 192). Stir in the chocolate 'polka dots' immediately, then pour into the prepared loaf tin.

5. While the fudge is still slightly warm, mark it into approximately 20 pieces, then allow it to become cool and firm before cutting and wrapping in lightly waxed paper.

Polka Dot Walnut Fudge

1. Follow recipe and method for Polka Dot Peanut Fudge.

2. Omit the peanut butter, use 3 tablespoons plain butter instead and 4 tablespoons chopped walnuts.

3. Finish as for Polka Dot Peanut Fudge.

Polka Dot Almond Fudge

1. Follow recipe and method for Polka Dot Peanut Fudge.

2. Omit the peanut butter, use 3 tablespoons plain butter instead and 4 tablespoons chopped roasted almonds.

3. Finish as for Polka Dot Peanut Fudge.

Polka Dot Hazelnut Fudge

1. Follow recipe and method for Polka Dot Peanut Fudge.

2. Omit the peanut butter, use 3 tablespoons plain butter instead and 4 tablespoons chopped roasted hazelnuts.

3. Finish as for Polka Dot Peanut Fudge.

Uncooked Almond Fudge

Makes approximately 1 lb (450 gm) fudge

EQUIPMENT

Electric mixer or wooden spoon
1 large mixing bowl
1 lightly greased 1 lb loaf tin
1 large sharp knife

Right: Rum creme fudge, Crème de Menthe fudge, uncooked fudge and fudge frosting on cake

INGREDIENTS

Imperial	Metric	Cup	Ingredient
3 oz	80 gm	3 oz	**Soft cream cheese**
2 oz	56 gm	½	**Chopped almonds**
Pinch	–	–	**Salt**
¼ teaspoon	–	–	**Almond essence**
14 oz	395 gm	2½	**Icing sugar**

METHOD

1. Put the cheese into the mixing bowl and beat either with an electric mixer or a wooden spoon until it is soft and creamy.
2. Gradually beat in all the remaining ingredients, then press the fudge into the prepared tin and chill until firm.
3. Cut into thin slices when required and wrap in lightly greased paper.

Chocolate and Almond Fudge

1. Follow recipe and method for Uncooked Almond Fudge.
2. Melt 2 oz (56 gm) plain chocolate in a small basin over a pan of hot water and beat this, along with the other ingredients, into the cream cheese.
3. Instead of pressing the mixture into the prepared tin, shape teaspoonfuls of the fudge into small balls and coat them with plain chocolate vermicelli.

Cherry and Almond Fudge

1. Follow recipe and method for Uncooked Almond Fudge.
2. Beat 2 oz (56 gm / ½ cup) finely chopped glacé cherries into the cream cheese along with the other ingredients.
3. Continue as for Uncooked Almond Fudge.

Uncooked Walnut Fudge

1. Follow recipe and method for Uncooked Almond Fudge but substitute chopped walnuts for the chopped almonds.
2. Complete as for Uncooked Almond Fudge.

Uncooked Coconut Fudge

1. Follow recipe and method for Uncooked Almond Fudge, substituting 4 tablespoons desiccated coconut for the chopped almonds.
2. Complete as for Uncooked Almond Fudge.

Fudge Layer

Makes approximately 1¾ lb (780 gm) fudge

EQUIPMENT

1 large heavy saucepan
1 metal tablespoon
1 wooden spoon
1 tablespoon
1 teaspoon
1 foil lined baking tray

44

INGREDIENTS

Imperial	Metric	Cup	Ingredient
12 oz	340 gm	1 ½	**Granulated sugar**
1	–	–	**Small can evaporated milk**
2 oz	56 gm	¼	**Butter**
6 oz	170 gm	6 oz	**Plain chocolate (grated)**
1 teaspoon	–	–	**Vanilla essence**
2 oz	56 gm	⅓	**Finely chopped peanuts**
3 oz	80 gm	½	**Peanut butter**

METHOD

1. Put the sugar and milk into the saucepan and heat gently, stirring continuously with the tablespoon until all the sugar has dissolved.

2. Bring the fudge to the boil and boil for 7 minutes, stirring from time to time to prevent the fudge from sticking to the bottom of the pan.

3. Remove the pan from the heat and stir in the butter and grated plain chocolate, then beat the fudge until it becomes smooth.

4. Add the vanilla essence and chopped peanuts.

5. Drop half the hot fudge from a tablespoon onto the foil lined baking tray, making about 20 drops in all.

6. Very quickly, using a teaspoon, put a little peanut butter onto each fudge drop and then cover this with spoonfuls of the remaining hot fudge mixture.

Note:
■ *These are a little difficult to wrap attractively because of the irregular shape, but they are so delicious that you will have no trouble in finding family and friends to eat them.*

Nutty Fudge Squares

Makes approximately 1 ¼ lb (560 gm) fudge

EQUIPMENT

1 large heavy saucepan
1 metal tablespoon
1 wooden spoon
1 sugar thermometer
1 lightly greased tin, 7 in (17 ½ cm) square
1 large sharp knife

INGREDIENTS

Imperial	Metric	Cup	Ingredient
1	–	–	**Small can evaporated milk**
1 lb	450 gm	2	**Granulated sugar**
1 tablespoon	–	–	**Golden syrup**
4 oz	112 gm	½	**Stoned chopped dates**
1 oz	30 gm	2 tablespoons	**Butter**
1 teaspoon	–	- -	**Vanilla essence**
2 oz	56 gm	½	**Finely chopped hazelnuts**

METHOD

1. Put the milk, sugar and golden syrup into the saucepan and heat gently, stirring all the time with the tablespoon to help the dissolving of the sugar crystals.
2. When the mixture reaches boiling point, add the chopped dates and continue cooking over a low heat to prevent the fudge from burning until the temperature reaches 238°F / 114°C, then remove from the cooker.
3. Add the butter but do not stir the fudge again. Allow it to cool to 110°F / 43°C, then add the vanilla essence and beat until the fudge starts to 'grain' (see page 192).
4. Pour the fudge into the prepared tin, sprinkle with the nuts and allow it to cool until firm. Wrap in lightly waxed paper.

Four-Minute Fudge

Makes approximately 1 ½ lb (675 gm) fudge

EQUIPMENT

1 large heavy saucepan
1 wooden spoon
1 lightly greased tin, 7 in (17 ½ cm) square

INGREDIENTS

Imperial	Metric	Cup	Ingredient
1	–	–	**Small can evaporated milk**
1 oz	30 gm	2 tablespoons	**Butter**
1 lb	450 gm	3	**Icing sugar**
6 oz	170 gm	–	**Plain chocolate**
3 oz	80 gm	–	**Marshmallows**

METHOD

1. Put the milk, butter and icing sugar into the saucepan and bring to the boil. Stir the mixture all the time to prevent it sticking to the bottom of the pan.
2. Boil the fudge for exactly 4 minutes, stirring occasionally.
3. Meanwhile, grate the chocolate and cut the marshmallows into pieces.
4. Add the chocolate and marshmallows to the fudge and beat, away from the heat, until the chocolate melts and the fudge thickens, then turn immediately into the prepared tin.
5. When the fudge is cool and firm, cut it into pieces about 1 in (2 ½ cm) square and wrap in lightly waxed paper.

Four-Minute Nut Clusters

1. Follow recipe and method for Four Minute Fudge.
2. After the fudge has been beaten and has thickened, add 2 oz (56 gm / ½ cup) chopped almonds, chopped walnuts or chopped hazelnuts.
3. Instead of turning it into a greased tin, drop the fudge from a teaspoon onto waxed paper and allow to cool and become firm.

Fudge Diagonals

Makes approximately 2 lb (900 gm) fudge

EQUIPMENT

1 large heavy saucepan
1 wooden spoon
1 sugar thermometer
1 large lightly greased plate
Waxed paper
1 large sharp knife

INGREDIENTS

Imperial	Metric	Cup	Ingredient
8 fl oz	240 ml	1	**Milk**
2 oz	56 gm	2 oz	**Plain chocolate**
2 tablespoons	–	–	**Golden syrup**
1½ lb	675 gm	3	**Granulated sugar**
Pinch	–	–	**Salt**
Pinch	–	–	**Cream of tartar**
1 oz	30 gm	2 tablespoons	**Butter**
1 teaspoon	–	–	**Vanilla essence**
2 oz	56 gm	½	**Chopped blanched almonds**

METHOD

1. Put the milk and the chocolate, cut into small pieces, into the saucepan. Heat gently until the chocolate has melted.

2. Stir in the golden syrup, sugar and salt, then cook over a medium heat, stirring continuously, until the sugar crystals have all dissolved.

3. Continue cooking without stirring until the temperature reaches 238°F / 114°C, then remove immediately from the heat.

4. Dissolve the cream of tartar in a very small amount of cold water, then very gently stir this into the mixture. Add the butter without stirring and allow the fudge to cool to lukewarm (110°F / 43°C).

5. Next add the vanilla essence and beat the fudge with a wooden spoon until it loses its gloss and starts to thicken. At this stage stir in the chopped nuts.

6. Turn the fudge onto the greased plate and leave until cool enough to handle and quite firm.

7. Divide in half and gently knead into two rolls about 2 in (5 cm) in diameter and about 5 in (12½ cm) long. Wrap these in waxed paper or foil, cool and chill thoroughly. Store in a cool place until required.

8. Present the fudge diagonally cut in ½ in (1¼ cm) slices and wrap in clear cellophane paper.

Walnut Fudge Diagonals

1. Follow recipe and method for Fudge Diagonals.

2. Add 2 oz (56 gm / ½ cup) chopped walnuts instead of the chopped almonds.

Coconut Fudge Diagonals

1. Follow recipe and method for Fudge Diagonals.

2. Add 4 tablespoons desiccated coconut instead of the chopped almonds.

Hazelnut Fudge Diagonals

1. Follow recipe and method for Fudge Diagonals.

2. Add 2 oz (56 gm / ½ cup) chopped hazelnuts instead of the chopped almonds.

Peanut Fudge Diagonals

1. Follow recipe and method for Fudge Diagonals.

2. Add 2 oz (56 gm / ½ cup) chopped peanuts instead of the chopped almonds.

Soft Chocolate Fudge

Makes approximately 1½ lb (675 gm) fudge

EQUIPMENT

1 large heavy saucepan
1 wooden spoon
1 sugar thermometer
1 lightly greased tin, 8 in (20 cm) square
1 large sharp knife

INGREDIENTS

Imperial	Metric	Cup	Ingredient
6 fl oz	180 ml	¾	**Milk**
3 oz	80 gm	3 oz	**Plain chocolate**
1 ½ lb	675 gm	3	**Granulated sugar**
Pinch	–	–	**Salt**
3 tablespoons	–	–	**Syrup**
3 oz	80 gm	⅓	**Butter**
1 ½ teaspoons	–	–	**Vanilla essence**

METHOD

1. Put the milk into the large pan and then add the chocolate, cut into small pieces.

2. Cook the milk and chocolate over a low heat until the milk has been well warmed through and the chocolate has melted.

3. Stir in the granulated sugar, salt and syrup, then raise the heat to medium and continue cooking until all the sugar has been dissolved. It is important to stir the mixture gently while it is heating so the milk does not burn; gentle stirring also hastens the dissolving of the sugar.

4. As soon as the sugar crystals have dissolved, cook the fudge mixture until the temperature reaches 236°F / 113°C, then remove immediately from the heat.

5. Add the butter, cut into small pieces and allow the mixture to cool, without stirring, to 110°F / 43°C.

6. At this stage add the vanilla essence and beat the fudge with the wooden spoon until it loses its gloss and starts to thicken. Pour immediately into the greased tin, but do not scrape the pan as, if any solid pieces of cooked fudge fall into the tin, they will solidify and cause the fudge to become very granular and sugary.

7. While the fudge is still warm, mark into squares and when it is completely cold, remove from the tin and cut into squares. Wrap in clear cellophane paper.

Nutty Soft Chocolate Fudge

1. Follow recipe and method for Soft Chocolate Fudge.

2. Add 4 tablespoons chopped almonds, hazelnuts or walnuts just before beating the fudge.

Soft Mocha Fudge

1. Follow recipe and method for Soft Chocolate Fudge.

2. Add 2 tablespoons powdered instant coffee to the warmed milk and chocolate mixture.

Soft Chocolate Raisin Fudge

1. Follow recipe and method for Soft Chocolate Fudge.

2. Add 4 tablespoons seedless raisins just before beating the fudge.

Soft Chocolate Pineapple Fudge

1. Follow recipe and method for Soft Chocolate Fudge.

2. Add 4 tablespoons chopped crystallized pineapple just before beating the fudge.

Soft Chocolate Ginger Fudge

1. Follow recipe and method for Soft Chocolate Fudge.

2. Add 4 tablespoons chopped stem ginger just before beating the fudge.

Soft Chocolate Cherry Fudge

1. Follow recipe and method for Soft Chocolate Fudge.

2. Add 4 tablespoons chopped glacé cherries just before beating the fudge.

48

Soft Apricot Fudge

1. Follow recipe and method for Soft Chocolate Fudge.

2. Add 4 tablespoons chopped dried apricots just before beating the fudge.

Marshmallow Chocolate Fudge

Makes approximately 2 lb (900 gm) fudge

EQUIPMENT

1 large heavy saucepan
1 wooden spoon
1 sugar thermometer
1 lightly greased tin, 8 in (20 cm) square
1 large sharp knife

INGREDIENTS

Imperial	Metric	Cup	Ingredient
1 lb	450 gm	2	**Granulated sugar**
2 oz	56 gm	¼	**Butter**
1 small can	–	–	**Evaporated milk**
6 oz	170 gm	–	**Dessert chocolate**
1 teaspoon	–	–	**Vanilla essence**
3 oz	80 gm	–	**Cut marshmallows**

METHOD

1. Put the sugar, butter and evaporated milk into the saucepan, and cook over a low heat, stirring continuously, until the temperature reaches 238°F / 114°C. Remove from the heat.

2. Grate the chocolate and add to the mixture together with the vanilla essence and cut marshmallows.

3. Beat until the grated chocolate melts and blends well with the mixture, then pour into the prepared tin and allow to cool just a little.

4. Mark into 1 in (2½ cm) squares, then wait until it is cold and firm before cutting and wrapping them in lightly waxed paper.

Crunchy Chocolate Fudge

Makes approximately 1 ¼ lb (560 gm) fudge

EQUIPMENT

1 large heavy saucepan
1 wooden spoon
1 sugar thermometer
1 lightly greased tin, 8 in (20 cm) square

INGREDIENTS

Imperial	Metric	Cup	Ingredient
4 fl oz	120 ml	½	**Single cream**
1 oz	30 gm	2 tablespoons	**Butter**
8 oz	225 gm	1	**Granulated sugar**
3 oz	80 gm	–	**Dessert chocolate, cut into pieces**
1 teaspoon	–	–	**Vanilla essence**
2 oz	56 gm	½	**Chopped walnuts**
4 oz	112 gm	1 ¼	**Digestive biscuit crumbs**
8 oz	225 gm	4	**Cut marshmallows**

METHOD

1. Put the cream, butter, sugar and chocolate pieces into the saucepan, bring to the boil over a moderate heat and heat until the sugar has dissolved. It is important to stir the mixture continuously as the chocolate and cream may scorch on the base of the pan.

2. As soon as the sugar has dissolved, raise the heat a little and continue cooking until the temperature reaches 238°F / 114°C. Remove from the heat.

3. Very quickly, stir in the vanilla essence, chopped walnuts, digestive biscuit crumbs and marshmallow, then pour the fudge into the prepared tin. Cool until firm then cut into 1 in (2½ cm) squares and wrap in lightly waxed paper.

Tip:

■ *If you are sending a parcel of fudge as a gift, then it is better to remove the whole slab from the tin, wrap it carefully in lightly waxed paper and send it this way rather than cutting it first. Cut fudge tends to get a light sugary coating which mars the traditional creaminess of fudge sweets.*

Maple Raisin Fudge

Makes approximately ½ lb (225 gm) fudge

EQUIPMENT

1 medium heavy saucepan
1 wooden spoon
1 sugar thermometer
Hand-held electric mixer
1 lightly greased 1 lb loaf tin

INGREDIENTS

Imperial	Metric	Cup	Ingredients
3 fl oz	90 ml	⅓	**Single cream**
8 fl oz	240 ml	1	**Maple syrup**
2 teaspoons	–	–	**Golden syrup**
½ teaspoon	–	–	**Vanilla essence**
2 oz	56 gm	½	**Seedless raisins**

METHOD

1. Put the cream, maple syrup and golden syrup into the saucepan, then cook over a low heat, stirring constantly, until the mixture starts to boil.

2. As soon as the mixture has boiled, continue cooking without stirring until the temperature reaches 238°F / 114°C.

3. Remove the pan from the heat, cool to 110°F / 43°C, then beat with a hand-held electric mixer until the mixture thickens. (This could take up to 15 minutes).

4. Add the vanilla essence and the raisins, then pour the fudge into the prepared loaf tin. Cool and then cut into about 10 pieces. Wrap in lightly waxed paper.

Tutti Frutti Fudge

Makes approximately 2 lb (900 gm) fudge

EQUIPMENT

1 large heavy saucepan
1 wooden spoon
Hand-held electric mixer
1 lightly greased tin, 9 in (22½ cm) square
1 large sharp knife

INGREDIENTS

Imperial	Metric	Cup	Ingredients
12 oz	*340 gm*	*1 ½*	**Granulated sugar**
4 tablespoons	*–*	*–*	**Golden syrup**
6 fl oz	*180 ml*	*¾*	**Single cream**
½ teaspoon	*–*	*–*	**Salt**
1 teaspoon	*–*	*–*	**Vanilla essence**
3 oz	*80 gm*	*¾*	**Chopped hazelnuts**
3 oz	*80 gm*	*¾*	**Chopped Brazil nuts**
3 oz	*80 gm*	*¾*	**Chopped walnuts**
4 oz	*112 gm*	*½*	**Chopped candied peel**
4 oz	*112 gm*	*½*	**Glacé cherries**

METHOD

1. Put the sugar, syrup, cream and salt into the saucepan and heat over a low heat, stirring continuously, until all the sugar crystals have dissolved.

2. Bring the syrup to the boil, cover the pan for about 1 minute, and then boil without the lid until the temperature reaches 238°F / 114°C.

3. Take the pan immediately from the heat, add the vanilla essence and then beat with the electric mixer for about 6 minutes until the fudge mixture becomes creamy and will hold its shape.

4. Mix in all the chopped fruit and nuts, with a wooden spoon and then turn into the prepared tin.

5. Chill in the refrigerator until the fudge is firm enough to cut, but allow it to remain in the refrigerator for 24 hours before serving. Cut into squares with a sharp knife.

West Country Honey Fudge

Makes approximately 1 ½ lb (675 gm) fudge

EQUIPMENT

1 large heavy saucepan
1 wooden spoon
1 sugar thermometer
1 lightly greased tin, 8 in (20 cm) square
1 large sharp knife

INGREDIENTS

Imperial	Metric	Cup	Ingredient
4 oz	112 gm	–	**Dessert chocolate**
4 fl oz	120 ml	½	**Evaporated milk**
8 oz	225 gm	1	**Granulated sugar**
6 oz	170 gm	1	**Soft brown sugar**
Pinch	–	–	**Salt**
4 tablespoons	–	–	**Devon honey or clear honey**
Pinch	–	–	**Baking powder**
2 oz	56 gm	¼	**Salted butter**

METHOD

1. Grate the chocolate, then put it, together with the milk, both types of sugar and salt into the saucepan.
2. Heat gently for about 5 minutes, stirring all the time to speed the dissolving of the sugar.
3. When the sugar crystals have completely dissolved, add the honey and baking powder.
4. Raise the heat a little so that the mixture comes to a low boil, then cook, stirring continuously, until the temperature reaches 238°F / 114°C. Remove from the heat.
5. Put the butter into the hot mixture, but do not stir at this stage. Allow the fudge to cool to 110°F / 43°C, then beat hard with a wooden spoon, until the mixture starts to 'grain' (see page 192). Turn into the prepared tin and mark into squares as the fudge begins to set.
6. When it is completely cold, remove from the tin, cut with a sharp knife and store in an airtight tin or wrap in lightly waxed paper.

Fudge Frosting

Makes enough to cover tops and sides of two 8 in (20 cm) layers of sponge cake

EQUIPMENT

1 large double boiler, or a large heavy based pan and a pudding basin which fits inside
1 wooden spoon
1 palette knife

INGREDIENTS

Imperial	Metric	Cup	Ingredient
6 oz	170 gm	–	**Plain chocolate chips or grated chocolate**
¾ oz	22 gm	1 ½ tablespoons	**Margarine**
3 fl oz	90 ml	⅓	**Golden syrup**
3 fl oz	90 ml	⅓	**Evaporated milk**
Pinch	–	–	**Salt**
1 lb	450 gm	3	**Icing sugar**

METHOD

1. Put the chocolate and margarine into the top pan of the double boiler, or into a pudding basin standing in a pan of hot water. (The water should come halfway up the sides of the basin). Stir with the wooden spoon until the ingredients melt.

2. Add the golden syrup, evaporated milk and salt. Mix well and then stir in the icing sugar, 4 or 5 tablespoons at a time.

3. Spread the fudge quickly over the sides and top of the sponge layers. Allow to cool thoroughly before cutting.

Orange Fudge Frosting

1. Follow recipe and method for Fudge Frosting.
2. Add 1 tablespoon orange juice and 1 tablespoon finely grated orange rind along with the syrup, evaporated milk and salt.

Coffee Fudge Frosting

1. Follow recipe and method for Fudge Frosting.
2. Add 1 tablespoon instant coffee dissolved in 1 tablespoon water along with the syrup, evaporated milk and salt.

Peppermint Fudge Frosting

1. Follow the recipe for Fudge Frosting.
2. Add a few drops peppermint essence before beating.

Rum Fudge Frosting

1. Follow the recipe for Fudge Frosting.
2. Add 1 tablespoon of rum before beating.

Brandy Fudge Frosting

1. Follow the recipe for Fudge Frosting.
2. Add 1 tablespoon of brandy before beating.

Liqueur Fudge Frosting

1. Follow the recipe for Fudge Frosting.
2. Add 1 tablespoon of any liqueur before beating.

Fudge Sauce

1. Follow recipe and method for Fudge Frosting, but increase the golden syrup and evaporated milk quantities to ¼ pt (150 ml/ ⅔ cup).
2. Serve hot over pudding, ice cream, etc.

Note:
■ *This can be stored in the refrigerator and then re-heated gently, but it must not boil again.*

3. Marzipan

Marzipan (almond paste) has been known and used for many years in the making of fine sweetmeats. The name, literally translated, means 'almond bread'.

As the base of marzipan is ground almonds, it has to be classed as one of the more expensive sweets. However, it can be cut and moulded into a variety of different shapes quite simply yet with a very professional result.

It is often worthwhile to make cooked marzipan, as this will keep longer than the uncooked variety. A good 'all-purpose' recipe for it is given below. If it is wrapped in wax paper and stored in a glass jar in a cool place, it will keep for quite a considerable time (up to a month). The marzipan is best coloured *before* storing as it is difficult to colour when cold and set.

If the marzipan becomes hard, add two or three drops of tepid water and knead thoroughly until pliable again. Wrap each coloured piece separately in waxed paper and store in a tin or box. Any good food colourings can be used. The best effect is achieved by moulding the natural almond paste and then painting the colours with a soft camel-hair brush.

Boiled Marzipan

Makes approximately 2 lb (900 gm) marzipan

EQUIPMENT

1 heavy based saucepan
1 metal tablespoon
1 wooden spoon
1 wooden board
1 sugar thermometer
Waxed paper
1 screw-top jar

INGREDIENTS

Imperial	Metric	Cup	Ingredients
1 lb	450 gm	2	**Granulated sugar**
8 fl oz	240 ml	1	**Water**
Pinch	–	–	**Cream of tartar, (dissolved in a little water)**
1 lb	450 gm	4	**Ground almonds**
10 drops (approx)	–	–	**Oil of ratafia or almond essence**

METHOD

1. Gently heat the sugar in the water, stirring gently with the tablespoon until completely dissolved.
2. Add the cream of tartar, bring to the boil and cook to 240°F / 116°C.
3. Remove from the heat and place the pan on a cool surface.
4. Add the ground almonds and ratafia or almond essence.
5. Stir very well until the mixture is well blended and creamy.
6. When it has cooled sufficiently to be handled, turn onto a board lightly dusted with icing sugar and knead until smooth. Colour some of it if required.

7. Flatten out the paste and leave until quite cold.
8. Wrap each coloured portion individually in waxed paper and pack in a closely covered jar or tin.
9. Leave for about one week in the refrigerator so that the flavour develops, then use as required or store in the refrigerator.

Note:
■ *For recipes for uncooked marzipan see page 192 (almond pâté). When making sweets which need a lot of moulding it is better to use the cooked marzipan as it is more pliable – uncooked marzipan tends to crack or become oily if it is kneaded too much.*

Marzipan Fruits and Flowers

Strawberries
Mould deep red marzipan flavoured with rosewater into strawberry shapes, then mould small leaves and a stalk out of green marzipan and press into the top.

Bananas
Mould yellow coloured marzipan into banana shapes and paint thin stripes of gravy browning on the bananas to give an authentic effect.

Oranges and Lemons
Colour marzipan orange and yellow and flavour with finely grated orange or lemon rind, or oil of orange or lemon. Mould into shape and press a whole clove into one end to form the brown stalk at the base of the fruit.

Pears
Model natural coloured marzipan into a pear shape and then paint pale pink colouring to give a 'blush' to the fruit. Use a whole clove to form the stalk at the base of the fruit and a piece of angelica for the stalk at the top.

Apples
Mould as for pears into a suitable shape and paint with green and red colouring. Use a clove to form the stem.

Flowers
For the more patient sweetmaker, the making of marzipan flowers can be very rewarding. Choose your flower shape (e.g. rose, chrysan-

themum, etc.) and decide on the colour. Each petal should be modelled individually and then carefully built up into the flower shape. Make stalks and leaves out of green coloured marzipan and arrange them around the flower head.

A simpler type of flower can be made out of natural marzipan and then painted afterwards, but for a really professional effect it is better to use the first method.

Note:
■ *Marzipan fruits can be arranged in small wicker baskets for presentation or packed into small brown paper bags. As they are best presented unwrapped, they should be eaten within a few days of making.*

Cherry Balls

1. Roll small amounts of boiled or unboiled marzipan into balls.
2. Press half a glacé cherry into the top of each one.
3. Roll in caster sugar and place in small white paper sweet cases.

Marzipan Filled Fruits

Coloured or plain marzipan can be used for filling fruits such as dates, apricots, prunes, etc. Always choose plump fruits, as dry ones will be rather tasteless.
1. Carefully remove the stones from the fruit and press a little marzipan into the cavity. If using dates or prunes, press the two halves together again so that they almost touch. If using apricots, leave in halves, or press the two halves together with the marzipan in the centre.
2. Roll in caster sugar and leave on a sheet of greaseproof paper to harden. Display in small fluted sweet cases.

Left: Marzipan filled prunes and stuffed apricots, cherry balls

Right: Marzipan fondants and fruits

Marzipan Fondants

EQUIPMENT

1 double boiler, or *a pudding basin standing in a pan of hot water*
1 small pudding basin

INGREDIENTS

Imperial	Metric	Cup	Ingredient
6 oz	170 gm	–	**Fresh Centre Fondant** (see page 15)
2 oz	56 gm	–	**Fresh marzipan**
Few drops	–	–	**Vanilla essence**
2 oz	56 gm	–	**Dessert chocolate**

METHOD

1. Warm the fondant in a double boiler or in a pudding basin over hot water.
2. Knead the fondant and the marzipan together.
3. Flavour with vanilla essence.
4. Melt the chocolate in a small basin over hot water and mix into the fondant / marzipan mixture. Knead until smooth and well blended.
5. Divide the mixture into four portions and mould each piece into a roll about ¼ in (a little under 1 cm) in diameter.
6. Cut each roll into pieces about 2 in (5 cm) long and wrap in coloured aluminium foil, or plain aluminium foil and coloured cellophane paper.

Marzipan Glaze

Marzipan sweets often look more professional if they are coated with the following glaze.

EQUIPMENT

1 double boiler, or *a pudding basin standing in a pan of hot water*
1 metal tablespoon
1 small saucepan
1 sugar thermometer
1 small sieve lined with muslin
1 tightly corked jar for storing

INGREDIENTS

Imperial	Metric	Cup	Ingredient
2 oz	56 gm	½	**Crushed gum arabic** (available at most chemists)
4 wineglasses	–	–	**Water**
4 cubes	–	–	**Sugar**
2 tablespoons	–	–	**White wine**

METHOD

1. Wash the crushed gum arabic and put it, together with 3 wineglasses of the water, into the top pan of the double boiler or into the basin standing in a pan of hot water. The water in the pan should be kept at boiling point and the gum stirred until it dissolves completely.

2. In a small saucepan dissolve the sugar cubes in the remaining wineglass of water. Boil the syrup to 228°F / 108°C.
3. Remove the pan from the heat. When the bubbles have died down, add the wine.
4. Leave the syrup to cool completely be-fore adding both to the gum, which must first be strained through a small sieve lined with muslin.
5. Store in a tightly corked bottle and use as required.

Moulding Marzipan Figures

Boiled marzipan can be moulded quite successfully into animal shapes, small figures and flowers. They can be made from pre-coloured marzipan, or made plain and then painted with a fine brush afterwards. The basic marzipan can also be rolled to about ¼ in thick and then cut out with metal cutters into animal, round or star shapes. Currants can be used to make eyes, thin string to make tails on mice and cats, and chocolate vermicelli to make spines on hedgehog shapes.

MARZIPAN FIGURES

Sleepy Duck

1. Mould the basic duck shape (Fig. 1) from about 4 oz (112 gm) of marzipan. Mould the head from a ball.
2. Colour a small piece of extra marzipan with red food colouring and roll this out very thinly. Cut a shallow triangular shape from this (Fig. 2) and fasten around the duck to make the shawl.

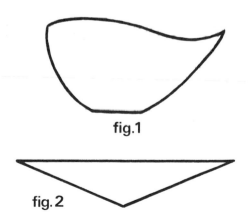

fig.1

fig.2

3. Using a fine paint brush and yellow food colouring, paint the beak yellow, and with brown food colour, paint in closed eyes and a narrow line down the centre of the beak.

4. Fix two white feathers under the shawl to represent wings, then allow the marzipan to harden overnight.
5. Glaze with marzipan glaze (see page 60) if required and wrap in clear cellophane paper

Nosy Hedgehog

1. Mould the basic hedgehog shape (Fig. 1) from about 2 oz. (56 gm) of marzipan.
2. Make the feet (Fig. 2) and press the hedgehog body onto them.
3. Paint the main part of the body with brown food colouring and press long pieces of chocolate vermicelli into the body to represent spines.

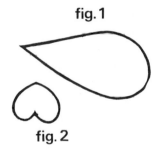

fig.1

fig.2

4. Paint two brown spots on the head to make the eyes, then make a very small round ball of marzipan and stick it onto the head, thus making the nose.
5. Paint the nose and feet with red food colouring and allow the marzipan to set overnight.
6. Glaze with marzipan glaze (see page 60) if required and wrap in cellophane.

Alfonso Toad

1. Mould the basic body shape out of 2 oz (56 gm) marzipan
2. Roll a thin piece of marzipan and fold in 2 places to make the legs.

Above: Moulding and colouring marzipan shapes

Right: Marzipan figures

---

3. Make the toes by splitting the foot end of the leg in two. Put one leg on each side of the body and carefully press them onto the body.

4. Roll two small balls and stick them onto the front of the head to make eyes.

5. Paint the whole toad with green food colouring, then paint a slit along the front of the eyes with dark brown food colouring.

6. Allow to harden overnight and then wrap in clear cellophane.

Psychedelic Caterpillar

1. Make 9 equally sized balls out of marzipan. Press them all together to form the cater-

pillar shape. At the tail end pull two points out from the marzipan to make the tail segment.

2. Colour the segments as follows with food colourings – the 3 tail segments, orange, the 2 centre segments, yellow and the 4 at the head end, green.

3. Press two mimosa balls into the head to make the eyes.

4. Allow the marzipan to harden and then wrap in clear cellophane.

Ladybird

1. Using 2 oz (56 gm) marzipan, mould a semicircular shape for the body of the ladybird. Mark the divisions down the centre of the back and around the base of the body with the back of a knife.

2. Make a small ball out of extra marzipan

62

to make the head and mould it gently onto the body.

3. Using a skewer, make two deep holes into the front of the head, then roll two very small pieces of marzipan to make the feelers. Press these into the holes and curve downwards to give a characteristic shape.

4. Colour the body deep red with food colouring, the head black or dark brown and the feelers yellow.

5. With a small extra piece of marzipan, mould the shape of an ivy leaf and mark veins on it with a knife. Paint it with dark green colour and when it has dried, place the finished ladybird on top

6. Allow the marzipan to harden and wrap in cellophane.

Mighty Mouse

1. Mould the body, head, legs and tail out of 4 oz (112 gm) white or pale yellow marzipan

2. Press the head gently onto the body and then press the legs in position, moulding them round to make the shape shown in the photograph.

3. Make two large ears and mould these onto the head.

4. Paint the insides of the ears with pale pink food colour, and the features onto the face with dark brown food colour. Use silver balls for the eyes.

5. Allow the mouse to harden and wrap in clear cellophane paper.

Toadstool

1. Make the stalk from 1 oz (30 gm) white or pale yellow marzipan (Fig. 1).

2. Make the top from a further 1 oz (30 gm) marzipan and paint it with red food colour.

3. Make 2 or 3 small spots out of white marzipan and flatten them onto the red coloured toadstool cap.

4. Gently press the finished cap onto the stalk and allow it to harden overnight.

5. Make a grass base out of shredded green tissue and wrap the toadstool in clear cellophane.

Note:
■ *Smaller toadstools can be made in the same way.*

4. Marshmallows

Marshmallows are made by pouring the boiling syrup onto dissolved gelatine and then adding stiffly beaten egg white. The resulting mixture is then beaten until very thick and white, and poured into a tin lined with greaseproof paper, then dredged with a mixture of icing sugar and cornflour. When set they can be cut into a number of different shapes and rolled in chopped nuts or toasted coconut, or dipped in chocolate.

Marshmallows

Makes approximately 1 ¼ lb (560 gm) marshmallows

EQUIPMENT

1 baking tin (medium size)
Greaseproof paper
1 large heavy saucepan
1 metal tablespoon
1 sugar thermometer
1 large mixing bowl
1 egg whisk
Fancy cutters

INGREDIENTS

Imperial	Metric	Cup	Ingredient
1 dessertspoon	–	–	*Icing sugar*
1 dessertspoon	–	–	*Cornflour*
½ pt	*300 ml*	*1 ¼*	*Water*
10 oz	*280 gm*	*1 ¼*	*Granulated sugar*
3 dessertspoons	–	–	*Powdered gelatine*
1	–	–	*Egg white*

METHOD

1. Sieve the icing sugar and cornflour, then line the baking tin with greaseproof paper and dredge it lightly with the sugar and cornflour mixture.

2. Put half the water and the granulated sugar into the saucepan and dissolve over a gentle heat, stirring with the metal tablespoon. Once the sugar crystals have completely dissolved, bring to the boil and continue to boil without stirring until the temperature registers 260°F / 127°C.

3. While the syrup is boiling up to the cor-

rect temperature, dissolve the gelatine with the rest of the water and whisk up the egg white very stiffly.

4. Put the dissolved gelatine in the large mixing bowl and pour the boiling syrup over it. Add any flavourings, (see flavouring suggestions on page 70) and whisk well.

5. Add the egg white and continue beating until the mixture is very thick and white. As soon as it reaches this stage, pour into the prepared tin and leave for 12 hours to set.

6. When the marshmallow is completely set, cut into rounds or fancy shapes and roll in icing sugar or one of the coatings suggested above, then leave for another 12 hours to dry.

Mixer Marshmallows

A simple recipe if you have an electric mixer. Makes approximately 1 lb (450 gm) marshmallows

EQUIPMENT

1 small pudding basin
1 large pan of boiling water
1 metal tablespoon
1 large mixing bowl
Electric mixer
1 prepared tin (see Marshmallow recipe above)
1 wooden board
1 sharp knife

Below: In the box are peppermint and chocolate marshmallows, on the plate assorted cherry and nut marshmallows

Left: Marshmallows being prepared

INGREDIENTS

Imperial	Metric	.Cup	Ingredient
2 dessertspoons	*–*	*–*	**Powdered gelatine**
2½ fl oz	*75 ml*	*⅓*	**Water**
4 oz	*112 gm*	*½*	**Granulated sugar**
5 fl oz	*150 ml*	*⅔*	**Glucose syrup**

METHOD

1.   Mix the gelatine and water in the small basin and allow it to soften. Place the basin in the pan of boiling water and stir until the gelatine has dissolved.

2.   Add the sugar and continue stirring with the tablespoon over the heat until the sugar has dissolved completely.

3.   Put the glucose syrup into the large mixing bowl, then add the gelatine and sugar mixture to the syrup and beat for about 15 minutes, or until the mixture is very thick and white.

4.   Pour the marshmallow into the prepared tin and smooth the top with a knife. Allow it to stand in a cool place, but not in the refrigerator, for about 1 hour until set, then remove the mass from the tin onto a wooden board, lightly dredged with the cornflour and icing sugar mixture (see previous Marshmallow recipe).

5.   Cut into squares with a sharp knife lightly wetted with cold water, then roll each portion in cornflour and icing sugar.

Note:
■ *Glucose syrup can be obtained from most chemists.*

COLOURINGS

Marshmallows can be coloured with normal vegetable food colourings, available at most department stores. The colourings should be added at the whisking stage before the marshmallow becomes too thick, so that the colour is evenly distributed.

Multi-coloured Marshmallows

1.   Follow either recipe for Marshmallows.
2.   Divide into two or three parts and colour each part differently as described above.
3.   As each is ready, pour into a prepared tin.
4.   Cool and finish as for Marshmallows.

Nut Marshmallows

1.   Follow either recipe for Marshmallows.
2.   Fold in 4 tablespoons chopped nuts before turning into the tin.
3.   Finish as for Marshmallows.

Raisin Marshmallows

1.   Follow either recipe for Marshmallows.
2.   Fold in 4 tablespoons seedless raisins before turning into the tin.
3.   Finish as for Marshmallows.

Date Marshmallows

1.   Follow either recipe for Marshmallows.
2.   Fold in 4 tablespoons chopped dates before turning into the tin.
3.   Finish as for Marshmallows.

Cherry Marshmallows

1.   Follow either recipe for Marshmallows.
2.   Fold in 4 tablespoons chopped maraschino or glacé cherries before turning into the tin.
3.   Finish as for Marshmallows.

Vanilla Marshmallows

1.   Follow either recipe for Marshmallows.
2.   Add 3 or 4 drops of vanilla essence at the whisking stage.
3.   Finish as for Marshmallows.

Lemon Marshmallows

1.   Follow either recipe for Marshmallows.
2.   Add 3 or 4 drops of lemon essence and 2 drops of yellow colouring at the whisking stage.
3.   Finish as for Marshmallows.

Orange Marshmallows

1.   Follow either recipe for Marshmallows.
2.   Add 1 dessertspoon of finely grated orange peel and 2 drops orange colouring at the whisking stage.
3.   Finish as for Marshmallows.

Peppermint Marshmallows

1.   Follow either recipe for Marshmallows.
2.   Add 3 drops of oil of peppermint and 2 drops green colouring at the whisking stage.
3.   Finish as for Marshmallows.

Rose Marshmallows

1.   Follow either recipe for Marshmallows.
2.   Add 1 teaspoon rosewater and 2 drops pink colouring at the whisking stage.
3.   Finish as for Marshmallows.

Chocolate Marshmallows

1.   Follow either recipe for Marshmallows.
2.   Add 3 tablespoons cocoa powder at the whisking stage.
3.   Finish as for Marshmallows.

Rainbow Marshmallows

1.   Follow either recipe for Marshmallows.
2.   After cutting, coat them in coloured granulated or caster sugar. To make this, put three drops of food colour into a large basin and toss white sugar in it until it becomes evenly coated.

Coconut Marshmallows

1.   Follow either recipe for Marshmallows
2.   After cutting, coat them in toasted or plain desiccated coconut.

Truffle Marshmallows

1.   Follow either recipe for Marshmallows.
2.   After cutting, coat them in plain or milk chocolate vermicelli.

5. Toffees

Toffee is basically a simple sugar mixture, but it needs to be boiled to a high temperature, and care should be taken with the cooking so that the mixture is kept perfectly clear. The following points will help in the making of good toffee:

a Use a little glucose or cream of tartar to prevent the toffee from becoming sugary and opaque.

b A large, heavy based pan must be used as toffee tends to boil over.

c Do not stir the toffee unless the recipe specifically states that you should. However, as the toffee might stick to the bulb of the thermometer and give an inaccurate reading, move it gently from time to time, but be careful not to agitate the syrup too much.

d After the temperature has reached 260°F / 127°C, keep the heat very low to pre-vent the toffee from boiling over. Remove the pan from the heat when the temperature is within a few degrees of the required figure, as the toffee will hold the heat and may become overcooked.

e As soon as the correct temperature is reached, pour the mixture into the prepared tin. The temperature of the toffee determines how brittle it will be when it is cooled. So toffees such as treacle toffee should be cooked to 270°F and peanut brittles, etc., to 300°F.

f If the toffee or similar sugar mixture is pulled while it is still warm it becomes opaque and has an attractive satin finish to it. A pair of well-oiled rubber gloves should be worn when handling the warm toffee, as it may still be hot enough to be uncomfortable.

Toffee

Makes approximately 1 ½ lb (675 gm) toffee

EQUIPMENT

1 large heavy saucepan
1 sugar thermometer
1 buttered tin, 12 in x 4 in (30 cm x 10 cm) or 6 in (15 cm) square.
1 large sharp knife

INGREDIENTS

Imperial	Metric	Cup	Ingredient
1 lb	*450 gm*	*2*	**Granulated sugar**
4 oz	*112 gm*	*½*	**Butter**
¼ pt	*150 ml*	*⅔*	**Water**
¼ level teaspoon	*–*	*–*	**Cream of tartar**

METHOD

1. Put all the ingredients into the pan and heat gently, without stirring, until dissolved.
2. Bring to the boil and cook until the temperature reaches 260°F / 127°C, then reduce the heat and continue heating until the syrup reaches 280°F / 138°C. Remove from the heat and pour immediately into the buttered tin.
3. When the toffee is almost set, mark into pieces with the sharp knife, then, when it is cold, it can be cut or broken quite easily.
4. Wrap in twists of lightly waxed paper and store in jars or airtight tins.

Peppermint Toffee

1. Follow recipe and method for Toffee.
2. Add ½ teaspoon peppermint essence just before the end of the cooking time.

Nut Toffee

1. Follow recipe and method for Toffee.
2. Add 4 oz. (112 gm / 1 cup) chopped walnuts or hazelnuts at the end of the cooking time.

Nut and Raisin Toffee

1. Follow recipe and method for Toffee.
2. Put 3 oz (80 gm / ¾ cup) chopped nuts and an equal amount of seedless raisins into the bottom of the tin before pouring the toffee into it.

Chocolate Toffee

1. Follow recipe and method for Toffee.
2. Add 4 oz (112 gm) grated dessert chocolate after the toffee has reached the correct temperature.
3. Stir well and finish as for Toffee.

Treacle Toffee

Makes approximately 1 ¼ lb (560 gm) treacle toffee

EQUIPMENT

1 large heavy saucepan
1 sugar thermometer
1 buttered tin, 12 in x 4 in (30 cm x 10 cm)
1 large sharp knife

INGREDIENTS

Imperial	Metric	Cup	Ingredient
1 lb	*450 gm*	*2½*	**Demerara sugar**
¼ pt	*150 ml*	*⅔*	**Water**
3 oz	*90 gm*	*⅓*	**Butter**
¼ level teaspoons	*–*	*–*	**Cream of tartar**
4 level tablespoons	*–*	*–*	**Black treacle**
4 level tablespoons	*–*	*–*	**Golden syrup**

METHOD

1. Put the sugar and water into the saucepan and dissolve gently over a low heat.
2. Add the remaining ingredients and bring the mixture slowly to the boil. Boil to

260°F / 127°C, then reduce the heat and continue cooking until the temperature reaches 270°F / 132°C.

3. Remove from the heat and pour into the prepared tin. When the toffee is almost set, mark in squares with a sharp knife so that the toffee can be cut or broken easily when completely cold.

Note:
■ *Treacle Toffee is traditionally eaten on Guy Fawkes night in England. It is usually broken into rough pieces with a wooden mallet and then handed round without being wrapped. However, for a more attractive finish it can be wrapped as toffees, in twists of lightly waxed paper.*

Toffee Honeycomb

Makes approximately 1 lb (450 gm) toffee

EQUIPMENT

1 large heavy saucepan
1 sugar thermometer
1 teacup
1 buttered tin, 12 in x 4 in (30 cm x 10 cm)

INGREDIENTS

Imperial	Metric	Cup	Ingredients
1 lb	450 gm	2	**Granulated sugar**
¼ pt	150 ml	⅔	**Water**
Pinch	–	–	**Cream of tartar**
3 tablespoons	–	–	**Golden syrup**
1 level teaspoon	–	–	**Bicarbonate of soda**
2 teaspoons	–	–	**Water**

METHOD

1. Put the sugar, water, cream of tartar and golden syrup into the saucepan and dissolve over a low heat, stirring gently with the thermometer.

2. Bring the mixture to the boil and heat to 260°F / 127°C, then reduce the heat and continue heating to 310°F / 154°C. Remove from the heat.

3. Blend the bicarbonate of soda with the 2 teaspoons water in the teacup and add to the toffee. Stir gently and pour at once into the tin.

4. When the toffee is nearly set, mark into pieces with the sharp knife, so that it can be broken easily when completely cold and set.

Note:
■ *Honeycomb toffee is very attractive if it is broken into rough shapes and packed in clear glass jars, but it should be eaten within a few days of making.*

Peppermint Toffee Honeycomb

1. Follow recipe and method for Toffee Honeycomb.

2. Blend 3 drops of oil of peppermint with the bicarbonate of soda and water before adding this to the toffee mixture.

Rum Toffee Honeycomb

1. Follow recipe and method for Toffee Honeycomb.

2. Blend 3 drops rum essence with the bicarbonate of soda and water before adding this to the hot toffee mixture.

Coffee Toffee Honeycomb

1. Follow recipe and method for Toffee Honeycomb.
2. Blend 1 tablespoon coffee essence with the bicarbonate of soda and water before adding this to the hot toffee mixture.

Almond Toffee Honeycomb

1. Follow recipe and method for Toffee Honeycomb.
2. Blend 3 drops almond essence with the bicarbonate of soda and water before adding this to the hot toffee mixture.

Vanilla Toffee Honeycomb

1. Follow recipe and method for Toffee Honeycomb.
2. Blend 3 drops vanilla essence with the bicarbonate of soda and water before adding to the hot toffee mixture.

Butterscotch

Makes approximately 1 lb (450 gm) butterscotch

EQUIPMENT

1 large heavy saucepan
1 wooden spoon
1 sugar thermometer
1 buttered tin, 7 in (13 cm) square
1 large sharp knife

INGREDIENTS

Imperial	Metric	Cup	Ingredients
1 lb	450 gm	2 ½	**Granulated sugar**
3 tablespoons	–	–	**Golden syrup**
3 oz	80 gm	⅓	**Butter**
3 tablespoons	–	–	**Water**
3 tablespoons	–	–	**Vinegar**

METHOD

1. Put all the ingredients into the saucepan and heat gently until dissolved.
2. Bring to the boil, stirring continuously, until the temperature reaches 300°F / 149°C, then pour immediately into the prepared tin.
3. Mark into squares with the sharp knife when the butterscotch is almost set.

Peanut Brittle

Makes approximately 1 ½ lb (675 gm) brittle

EQUIPMENT

1 large heavy pan
1 sugar thermometer
1 buttered tin, 12 in x 4 in (30 cm x 10 cm)
1 large sharp knife

INGREDIENTS

Imperial	Metric	Cup	Ingredients
4 oz	112 gm	½	*Granulated sugar*
6 oz	160 gm	1	*Soft brown sugar*
6 tablespoons	–	–	*Golden syrup*
¼ pt	150 ml	⅔	*Water*
2 oz	56 gm	¼	*Butter*
¼ level teaspoon	–	–	*Bicarbonate of soda*
12 oz	340 gm	1½	*Chopped unsalted peanuts, slightly warmed*

METHOD

1. Put both types of sugar, the syrup and the water into a large heavy pan and dissolve over a low heat.
2. Add the butter and bring the mixture to the boil. Boil until the temperature reaches 260°F / 126°C, then reduce the heat and continue cooking until the temperature registers 300°F / 150°C.
3. Add the bicarbonate of soda and the warmed nuts, then pour the mixture slowly into the tin. Mark into bars with the knife when the brittle is almost set.
4. Wrap in waxed paper or store in an airtight jar.

French Almond Brittle

Makes approximately 1 ½ lb (675 gm) brittle

EQUIPMENT

1 buttered tin, 12 in x 4 in (30 cm x 10 cm)
1 large heavy pan
1 sugar thermometer

INGREDIENTS

Imperial	Metric	Cup	Ingredient
4 oz	112 gm	1	*Blanched almonds*
1 lb	450 gm	2	*Granulated sugar*
6 fl oz	180 ml	¾	*Water*
Pinch	–	–	*Cream of tartar*

METHOD

1. Put the almonds into a warm oven to dry them out and brown them slightly, then arrange them over the base of the tin.
2. Put the sugar and water into the saucepan and heat gently until the sugar has dissolved.
3. Bring the syrup to the boil and cook until

Following pages:
Left: Basic toffee, peppermint and treacle toffee

Right: Butterscotch, toffee and peppermint honeycomb

the thermometer registers 260°F / 127°C. Add the cream of tartar, then reduce the heat and cook until the temperature reaches 310°F / 154°C.

4. Pour the toffee over the nuts and allow to cool and set completely before breaking the toffee into pieces and storing in an airtight tin.

Toffee Apples

Makes 6-8 apples

EQUIPMENT

1 large heavy based saucepan
1 sugar thermometer
6-8 thin wooden or paper lollipop sticks
1 greased baking tray

INGREDIENTS

Imperial	Metric	Cup	Ingredient
1 lb	*450 gm*	*2*	**Demerara sugar**
2 oz	*56 gm*	*¼*	**Butter**
2 teaspoons	*–*	*–*	**Vinegar**
¼ pt	*150 ml*	*⅔*	**Water**
6-8			**Apples, medium-sized**

METHOD

1. Put the sugar, butter, vinegar, water and golden syrup into the saucepan.
2. Heat the ingredients gently until the sugar dissolves, then boil rapidly until the temperature reaches 290°F / 143°C.
3. While the syrup is coming up to the correct temperature, wipe the apples and push the sticks into the cores.
4. Dip the apples quickly into the toffee, twirl round for a few seconds, then stand on the greased baking sheet until set.

Note:
■ *Toffee apples are traditionally wrapped in coloured cellophane and can then be presented in a wicker basket, or arranged in a suitably sized glass pot or jar.*

PULLED SWEETS

Pulled Toffee

1. Follow recipe and method for Toffee.
2. Pour the finished mixture onto a baking sheet and allow it to become fairly cool.
3. Take the sides of the mixture and fold over towards the middle as quickly as possible, then pull, fold back and pull again until the toffee becomes opaque.
4. Cut into even pieces and wrap in waxed paper.

New Jersey Taffy

This is an old recipe for the coloured 'taffy' which is sold during the summer in New Jersey. The taffy is coloured and flavoured and then cut and wrapped in twists of waxed or cellophane paper.
Makes approximately 1 ½ lb (675 gm) taffy

82

EQUIPMENT

1 large heavy pan
1 sugar thermometer
1 buttered baking sheet
Scissors

INGREDIENTS

Imperial	Metric	Cup	Ingredient
1 lb	450 gm	2	**Granulated sugar**
¼ pt	150 ml	⅔	**Glucose syrup**
8 fl oz	240 ml	1	**Water**
3 tablespoons	–	–	**Cornflour**
1 oz	30 gm	2 tablespoons	**Butter**
1 teaspoon	–	–	**Salt**

METHOD

1. Mix all the ingredients together and put them into a large saucepan.

2. Bring to the boil, stirring continuously, and cook to 260°F / 127°C. Stir well, then add flavouring and colouring as required. Pour onto the baking sheet and allow to cool until it can be handled comfortably.

3. Take the sides of the mixture and fold towards the centre, then pull, fold back and pull again until the taffy is silky and opaque.

4. Pull the piece of taffy out into a rope about ½ in (1 ¼ cm) in diameter, then cut into pieces about 1 ½ in (4 cm) long. Wrap in lightly waxed paper and twist the ends.

Strawberry Taffy

1. Follow recipe and method for New Jersey Taffy.

2. Add a few drops of strawberry essence and pink colouring.

Peppermint Taffy

1. Follow recipe and method for New Jersey Taffy.

2. Add a few drops of peppermint essence and green colouring.

Orange Taffy

1. Follow recipe and method for New Jersey Taffy.

2. Add 1 dessertspoon finely grated orange peel and orange colouring.

Lemon Taffy

1. Follow recipe and method for New Jersey Taffy.

2. Add 1 dessertspoon finely grated lemon peel and yellow colouring.

Vanilla Taffy

1. Follow recipe and method for New Jersey Taffy.

2. Add a few drops vanilla essence.

Aniseed Taffy

1. Follow recipe and method for New Jersey Taffy.

2. Add a few drops of oil of aniseed.

Coloured Sugar Sticks

Makes approximately 2½ lb (1,125 gm)
sugar sticks

Above: Pink and green taffy, pulled taffy

Right: Toffee apples and ingredients

EQUIPMENT

1 large heavy saucepan
1 sugar thermometer
1 buttered baking sheet
Scissors
Food colourings

INGREDIENTS

Imperial	Metric	Cup	Ingredient
2 lb	900 gm	4	**Granulated sugar**
1 small teaspoon	–	–	**Cream of tartar**
12 fl oz	360 ml	1½	**Water**
¼ teaspoon	–	–	**Tartaric acid**

METHOD

1. Put all the ingredients except the colouring into the saucepan, then dissolve the sugar slowly over a low heat.
2. Bring quickly to the boil and boil to 310°F / 154°C. Pour the mixture immediately onto the buttered baking sheet and allow to cool.
3. At this stage the colouring should be added – approximately 5 drops for this amount of candy. Roll and pull as for Pulled Toffee (page 82).
4. When the mixture is semi-opaque, roll into sticks, cut into pieces about 5 in (13 cm) long and allow to cool and set.

Note:
■ *To make striped sticks, have two colours of candy, fold together and twist before cutting. A combination of pink and white is most usual, but of course other colour combinations can be used.*

Walking Sticks

1. Follow recipe and method for Coloured Sugar Sticks.
2. At the point where the candy is cut, shape one end into a semi-circular curve to make the handle of the walking stick. Allow to set.

Candy Hoops

1. Follow the recipe and method for Coloured Sugar Sticks.
2. At the point where the candy is cut, shape the cut length into a circle and press the ends together. Allow to cool and set.

Edinburgh Rock

Makes approximately 2 ½ lb (1125 gm) rock

EQUIPMENT

1 large heavy saucepan
1 sugar thermometer
1 buttered saucepan
1 bowl of cold water
1 large knife

INGREDIENTS

Imperial	Metric	Cup	Ingredient
2 lb	900 gm	4	**Granulated sugar**
½ pt	300 ml	1 ¼	**Water**
¼ teaspoon	–	–	**Cream of tartar**
2 teaspoons	–	–	**Tartaric acid**

METHOD

1. Put the sugar and water into the pan and heat slowly until the sugar dissolves completely.
2. Bring the syrup to the boil and then add the cream of tartar, dissolved in 1 teaspoon water. Boil to 280°F / 138°C, then remove from the heat and pour immediately into the greased pan.
3. Put the pan into the bowl of cold water. Colour and flavour at this stage. Add the tartaric acid to give the characteristic taste.
4. Fold the mixture as described in the Pulled Toffee recipe (page 82), then pull, fold and pull until thick and creamy. Divide into long thin pieces, and cut into 4-6 in (10-15 cm) lengths with the blunt edge of a knife. Flatten with the back of the knife and leave exposed to the air for several days.

Lemon Flavoured Edinburgh Rock

1. Follow recipe and method for Edinburgh Rock.
2. Colour with 2 drops of yellow colouring and add 2 teaspoons of lemon essence or 1 tablespoon finely grated lemon peel.

Orange Flavoured Edinburgh Rock

1. Follow recipe and method for Edinburgh Rock.
2. Colour with 2 or 3 drops of orange colouring and flavour with 2 teaspoons orange essence or 1 tablespoon finely grated orange peel.

Ginger Flavoured Edinburgh Rock

1. Follow recipe and method for Edinburgh Rock.
2. Flavour with 1 teaspoon powdered ginger.

Peppermint Flavoured Edinburgh Rock

1. Follow recipe and method for Edinburgh Rock.
2. Flavour with 1 small teaspoon peppermint essence and colour with 2 or 3 drops green colouring.

Vanilla Flavoured Edinburgh Rock

1. Follow recipe and method for Edinburgh Rock.
2. Flavour with 1 small teaspoon vanilla essence and leave the colour white.

Raspberry Flavoured Edinburgh Rock

1. Follow recipe and method for Edinburgh Rock.
2. Colour with 3 or 4 drops pink or red colouring and flavour with 2 small teaspoons raspberry essence.

Strawberry Flavoured Edinburgh Rock

1. Follow recipe and method for Edinburgh Rock.
2. Colour with 2 or 3 drops red colour and flavour with 1½ teaspoons strawberry essence.

Rose Flavoured Edinburgh Rock

1. Follow recipe and method for Edinburgh Rock.
2. Flavour with 2 teaspoons rosewater and colour with 2 drops pink colouring.

Note:
■ *If you are using only, say, ¼ of the rock recipe, reduce the flavouring and colouring accordingly.*

Following pages:
Left: Toffee apples and peanut brittle

Right: Sugar sticks and Edinburgh rock

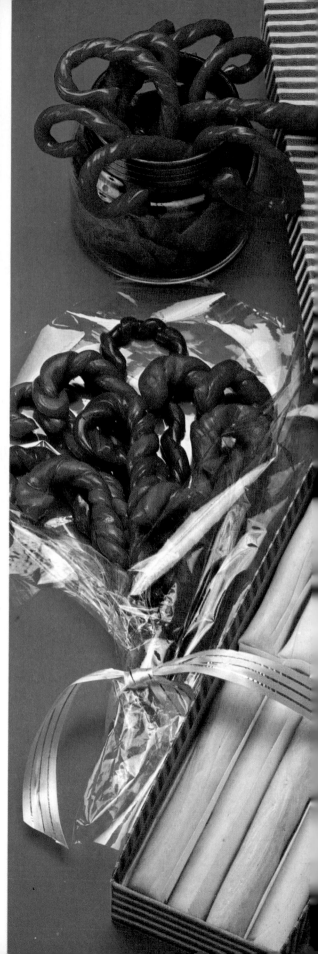

6. Butter Sweets

Sweets made with butter generally fall between the categories of toffees and brittle. Butter crunches can be the most delicious of all sweetmeats but the recipes must be followed very carefully indeed and it is very important to use a thick, heavy based pan of a material such as cast iron, which will retain the heat. The sugar and butter mixture must be at a regular temperature throughout, otherwise it will boil where the pan is hottest, at the base, and then chill at the top of the pan. This will result in a mass of cooked sugar lumps floating in boiling butter once it has boiled. The stirring of the candy must be constant right to the point of the candy being cooked, so that all the sugar is kept in motion with all the butter all the time.

Another important aspect is the chopping of the nuts. The nuts in the centre should be very coarsely chopped, whilst those on the outside, if used, should be finely chopped. Although it is rather a tedious procedure, the finely chopped nuts should really be chopped with a large knife. They can be put in a food blender, but take care not to over-chop them otherwise they will become oily.

The whole process of making butter sweets sounds tedious, but the result is well worth the effort.

Golden Butter Crunch

Makes approximately 2 lb (900 gm) butter crunch

EQUIPMENT

1 large heavy saucepan
1 wooden spoon
1 buttered tin, 8 in x 10 in (20 cm x 25 cm)
1 sugar thermometer
1 large sharp knife

INGREDIENTS

Imperial	Metric	Cup	Ingredient
1¼ lb	*560 gm*	*2½*	**Granulated sugar**
8 fl oz	*240 ml*	*1*	**Water**
4 oz	*112 gm*	*¾*	**Glucose**
4 oz	*112 gm*	*½*	**Butter**
3 drops	*–*	*–*	**Vanilla essence**

METHOD

1. Dissolve the sugar in the water over a low heat, then stir in the glucose and bring the mixture quickly to the boil stirring continuously.

2. Continue boiling and stirring until the

temperature registers 290°F / 143°C, then remove from the heat and drop the butter into the hot syrup a small piece at a time and stir until melted and incorporated. Return to the heat and boil without stirring for 1 minute.

3. Add the vanilla and pour immediately into the prepared tin and allow to cool.

4. When the crunch is almost set, mark into squares with the sharp knife so that it can be cut or broken easily when cold. Store in air-tight jars and then wrap in coloured cellophane paper whenever required.

Peanut Butter Crunch

1. Follow recipe and method for Golden Butter Crunch, substituting crunchy peanut butter for the butter.

2. Finish as for Golden Butter Crunch.

Almond Butter Crunch

1. Follow recipe and method for Golden Butter Crunch.

2. Add 4 tablespoons chopped toasted almonds with the vanilla essence.

3. Finish as for Golden Butter Crunch.

Buttered Almonds

Makes approximately 12 oz (340 gm) buttered almonds

EQUIPMENT

1 well greased baking sheet
1 large heavy pan
1 metal dessertspoon
1 sugar thermometer

Below: Buttered almonds and brazils

Right: Golden butter crunch, walnut crunch, chocolate-coated and plain crunch and almond butter crunch

INGREDIENTS

Imperial	Metric	Cup	Ingredient
2 oz	56 gm	½	**Almonds**
8 oz	225 gm	1 ¼	**Soft light brown sugar**
¼ pt	150 ml	⅔	**Water**
Pinch	–	–	**Cream of tartar**
2 oz	56 gm	¼	**Butter**

METHOD

1. Blanch the almonds by standing them in boiling water for a few minutes and then remove the skins. Warm them in a very low oven and then place them on the greased baking sheet, allowing a little space in between each nut.

2. Put the sugar and water into the saucepan and dissolve over a gentle heat. Bring to the boil, add the remaining ingredients and boil to 280°F / 138°C.

3. Remove the syrup from the heat and quickly spoon a little over each nut. Allow to set. Store the nuts in an airtight tin and wrap in coloured cellophane when required.

Buttered Brazil Nuts

1. Follow recipe and method for Buttered Almonds.

2. Substitute brazil nuts for almonds.

Chocolate Coated Walnut Butter Crunch

Makes approximately 1 ¼ lb (560 gm) butter crunch

EQUIPMENT

1 large heavy pan
1 wooden spoon
1 large buttered baking sheet
1 sugar thermometer
1 palette knife
1 small basin
Waxed paper

INGREDIENTS

Imperial	Metric	Cup	Ingredient
8 oz	225 gm	1	**Butter**
8 oz	225 gm	1	**Granulated sugar**
1 tablespoon	–	–	**Glucose syrup**
¼ teaspoon	–	–	**Salt**
2 oz	56 gm	½	**Coarsely chopped walnuts**
4 oz	112 gm	1	**Finely chopped walnuts**
4 oz	112 gm	–	**Milk chocolate**

METHOD

1. Melt the butter in the saucepan over a high heat, then add the sugar slowly, stirring all the time.
2. As soon as the mixture boils, add the glucose syrup and cook to 290°F / 143°C, stirring continuously.
3. Add the salt and the coarsely chopped nuts when the correct temperature is reached, then pour immediately onto the buttered baking sheet.
4. Spread the mixture with the palette knife and allow to cool and set.

5. Remove the walnut crunch from the baking sheet, trying to keep it all in one piece, and place it on a wire cooling rack over a sheet of waxed paper.
6. Melt the chocolate in the basin over a pan of hot water, and then pour it over the nut crunch so that the top and sides are completely covered.
7. Quickly sprinkle the top with the finely chopped walnuts and allow to cool and set. Break into suitably sized pieces and store in flat boxes between layers of waxed paper.

Walnut Butter Crunch (plain)

1. Follow recipe and method for Chocolate Coated Walnut Crunch, omitting points 5, 6 and 7.
2. When the crunch has hardened, break it into mouth-sized pieces and store in flat boxes between layers of waxed paper.

7. Nougat

Nougat is a firm chewy sweet which originated in France. It is sold as plain bars and can also be used as a centre for chocolates. A wide variety of assorted chopped dried fruits and nuts (but not peanuts) give additional flavour and an attractive appearance to the nougat.

Nougat

Makes approximately 1 ½ lb (675 gm) nougat

EQUIPMENT

1 large heavy saucepan
1 sugar thermometer
1 large bowl of cold water
1 egg whisk
1 wooden spoon
1 tin, 8 in (20 cm) square, lined with rice paper

INGREDIENTS

Imperial	Metric	Cup	Ingredient
12 oz	340 gm	1 ½	**Granulated sugar**
2 oz	56 gm	½	**Powdered glucose**
3 fl oz	90 ml	⅓	**Water**
4 tablespoons	–	–	**Clear honey**
2	–	–	**Egg whites**
4 oz	112 gm	1	**Chopped roasted almonds**
2 tablespoons	–	–	**Chopped angelica**
2 tablespoons	–	–	**Chopped glacé cherries**
Few drops	–	–	**Vanilla essence**

METHOD

1. Dissolve the sugar and glucose in the water, add the honey, then bring to the boil and boil to 280°F / 138°C. Remove the pan from the heat and place in the bowl of cold water until the bubbles subside.

2. Meanwhile beat the egg whites until stiff. When the bubbles have gone from the syrup, add the beaten whites, nuts, angelica, cherries and vanilla essence. Stir until thick and firm.

Left: Soft Italian nougat, a box of cashew nougat special, chocolate nougat

3. Turn the nougat into the lined tin, then cover with more rice paper and leave to cool and set.
4. When the nougat is cold, cut into bars or squares and wrap in cellophane paper. The nougat can also be coated or dipped in chocolate (see page 151).

Chocolate Nougat

1. Follow recipe and method for Nougat.
2. Add 2 oz (56 gm) grated plain chocolate with the fruit and nuts.
3. Finish as for Nougat.

Soft Italian Nougat

Makes approximately 2 lb (900 gm) nougat

EQUIPMENT

1 medium sized mixing bowl
2 wooden spoons
1 small saucepan
1 metal tablespoon
1 lightly greased tin, 12 in x 4 in (30 cm x 10 cm)
1 palette knife
1 sharp knife

INGREDIENTS

Imperial	Metric	Cup	Ingredient
6 oz	170 gm	1 ¼	**Unsalted butter**
4 oz	112 gm	1	**Cocoa powder**
6 oz	170 gm	¾	**Granulated sugar**
6 oz	170 gm	1	**Ground almonds**
1 **whole egg** + 1 **egg yolk** (lightly beaten together)			
6 oz	170 gm	6 oz	**Petit beurre biscuits**

METHOD

1. Soften the butter, then beat in the cocoa powder until it resembles a soft paste.
2. Melt the sugar with a little water in the saucepan, then beat it into the cocoa and almond mixture as soon as the sugar has dissolved, alternating with the ground almonds.
3. Stir in the eggs, then finally break the biscuits into small almond-sized pieces and fold them carefully through the chocolate mixture. The pieces should remain whole.
4. Turn the mixture into the prepared tin and carefully smooth it over with a palette knife.
5. Chill in the coolest part of the refrigerator, preferably overnight, then cut into squares. Serve chilled as it can become sticky.

French Nougat

Makes approximately 1 lb (450 gm) nougat

EQUIPMENT

1 medium sized saucepan
1 egg whisk
1 metal tablespoon
1 wooden spoon
1 lightly greased shallow tin, 6 in x 4 in (15 cm x 10 cm)

INGREDIENTS

Imperial	Metric	Cup	Ingredient
8 oz	225 gm	1	**Clear honey**
1	–	–	**Egg white**
6 oz	170 gm	¾	**Chopped almonds**
2 tablespoons	–	–	**Chopped hazelnuts**
2 tablespoons	–	–	**Chopped glacé cherries**

METHOD

1. Put the honey into the saucepan and boil until a drop solidifies immediately it is dropped onto a cold plate. It is important that the honey solidifies, otherwise the nougat will not set.
2. Reduce the heat to a simmer, whisk the egg white until it is stiff, then fold it through the honey until it is evenly mixed.
3. Remove the pan from the heat, stir in the chopped nuts and chopped cherries, then turn into the lightly greased tin and refrigerate until firm enough to cut.
4. Cut into squares or bars and either place in fluted paper sweet cases or wrap in thin cellophane paper.

Note:
■ *If you wish, when making any type of nougat you can line the tin with rice paper which facilitates handling.*

American Double Nougat

Makes approximately 5 lb (2,250 gm) nougat

EQUIPMENT

1 large heavy saucepan
1 metal tablespoon
1 sugar thermometer
1 egg whisk
1 wooden spoon
1 large mixing bowl
1 lightly greased tin, 9 in (22½ cm) square
1 large sharp knife

INGREDIENTS

Imperial	Metric	Cup	Ingredient
Mixture 1:			
1 fl oz	30 ml	⅛	**Water**
6 oz	170 gm	¾	**Granulated sugar**
5 fl oz	150 ml	⅔	**Golden syrup**
1	–	–	**Large egg white**
Mixture 2:			
8 fl oz	240 ml	1	**Golden syrup**
12 oz	340 gm	1 ½	**Granulated sugar**
1 oz	30 gm	2 tablespoons	**Butter**
1 ½ teaspoons	–	–	**Vanilla essence**
pinch	–	–	**Salt**
6 oz	170 gm	¾	**Chopped almonds or almonds and hazelnuts mixed**

METHOD

Mixture 1

1. Put the water, sugar and syrup into the saucepan and cook gently over a low heat, stirring continuously until all the sugar has dissolved.

2. Bring the sugar solution to the boil, then reduce the heat and continue cooking until the thermometer registers 280°F / 138°C.

3. Just before the required temperature is reached, beat the egg whites until stiff and then pour the sugar syrup onto the whipped egg whites, beating constantly, preferably with an electric hand mixer, until the mixture is thick and just lukewarm. At this stage it can be kept for several days in the refrigerator if it is well covered with waxed paper.

Mixture 2

4. Put the syrup and sugar into a large heavy saucepan and heat gently, stirring continuously, until the sugar crystals have dissolved. Raise the heat to medium and cook, still stirring continuously, until the temperature reaches 275°F / 135°C.

Combining the mixtures

5. While Mixture 2 is being prepared, put the completed Mixture 1 into a large, lightly greased mixing bowl. Pour all the hot Mixture 2 over it, then mix with a wooden spoon. Slowly add the butter and vanilla essence and continue mixing until all the ingredients are thoroughly combined.

6. Add the salt and the chopped nuts and mix again. Stir till cool and thick then turn into the prepared tin and flatten with the hands.

7. After the mixture has stood for several hours, turn it onto a cutting board and cut into small squares 1 in (2 ½ cm) in diameter. Wrap in waxed paper.

Cashew Nougat Special

Makes approximately 1 lb (450 gm) nougat

EQUIPMENT

1 large heavy saucepan
1 metal tablespoon
1 sugar thermometer
1 egg whisk
1 electric mixer
1 wooden spoon
1 lightly greased tin, 8 in (20 cm) square
Scissors

Right: A box of French nougat, also plain nougat and soft Italian nougat

INGREDIENTS

Imperial	Metric	Cup	Ingredient
6 fl oz	180 ml	¾	*Golden syrup*
8 oz	225 gm	1	*Sugar*
3 fl oz	90 ml	⅓	*Water*
1	–	–	*Egg white*
1 ½ tablespoons	–	–	*Honey*
3 tablespoons	–	–	*Chopped glacé cherries*
3 tablespoons	–	–	*Chopped cashew nuts*

METHOD

1. Put the syrup, sugar and water into the saucepan. Cook over a gentle heat, stirring continuously, until the sugar has dissolved, then raise the temperature slightly and cook to 285°F / 141°C.

2. Just before the correct temperature is reached, beat the egg white until really stiff, then fold in the honey.

3. Pour the hot syrup mixture over the egg white and beat continuously, with an electric mixer for preference, until the mixture thickens considerably and loses its gloss.

4. Stir in the chopped cherries and the cashew nuts, then pour the nougat into the greased pan, cool and cover. It is best if you can allow the nougat to stand in the refrigerator for a few days before it is cut.

5. To cut the nougat, divide it into eight strips then remove each strip from the pan. Cut each strip with a pair of scissors and wrap the pieces in light cellophane paper.

8. Jellies and Turkish Delight

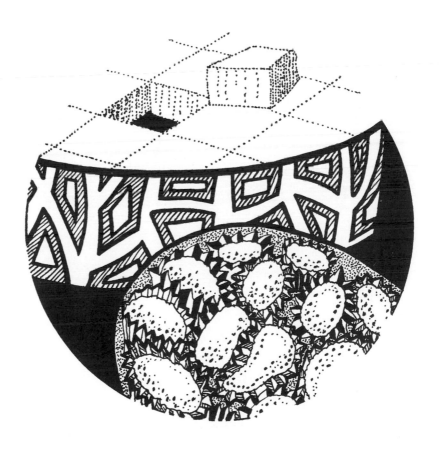

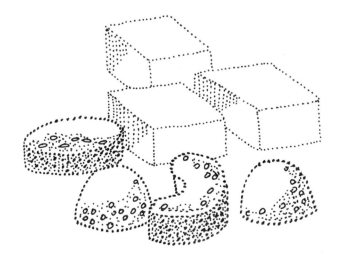

Jellies are attractive, varied and on the whole, quite simple to make. They are set by adding gelatine, gum arabic, arrowroot and cornflour. Alternatively a fruit pulp can be reduced with sugar until stiff enough to set firmly. They are best poured into shallow metal tins, and they can then be cut out with fancy cutters into attractive shapes.

Finish the jellies in one of the following ways:

a   Dampen and roll them in caster, granulated or coloured sugar.

b   Roll them in icing sugar and cornflour mixed in equal quantities.

c   Roll them in icing sugar alone.

d   Coat them in chocolate.

All jellies, when finished, are best if they are left for twenty-four hours in the air. They should then be packed with a mixture of icing sugar and cornflour between the layers in airtight boxes lined with greaseproof paper. As they do not keep very well, they should not be stored for an indefinite period.

Fresh Fruit Jellies

Makes approximately 12 oz (340 gm) jellies

EQUIPMENT

1 large heavy pan
1 metal tablespoon
1 tin, 6 in (15 cm) square
Fancy cutters

INGREDIENTS

Imperial	Metric	Cup	Ingredients
¼ pt	150 ml	⅔	**Fruit juice (orange, lemon, blackcurrant)**
3½ oz	95 gm	½	**Granulated sugar**
6 tablespoons	–	–	**Glucose**
2 tablespoons	–	–	**Powdered gelatine**

METHOD

1.   Put the fruit juice and sugar into the pan and heat gently until the sugar has dissolved, stirring all the time.

2.   Add the glucose and gelatine and continue heating gently until the gelatine has dissolved.

3. Pour the mixture into the tin, which should be lightly wetted, and allow the jelly to set completely.

4. Turn the jelly out and cut into cubes or fancy shapes (orange and lemon crescent shapes, etc.) and finish in one of the ways mentioned above.

■ *An attractive gift, especially for children, is a box of assorted jellies displayed in small paper cases.*

Peach Jellies

Makes approxmately 1 ½ lb (675 gm) jellies

EQUIPMENT

1 large heavy pan
1 metal tablespoon
1 wooden spoon
1 tin, 8 in (20 cm) square

INGREDIENTS

Imperial	Metric	Cup	Ingredient
½ pt	300 ml	1 ¼	**Peach purée (made from 1 medium can of peaches)**
1 lb	450 gm	2	**Granulated sugar**
½ oz packet	15 gm	–	**Powdered gelatine**
1 packet	–	–	**Orange jelly**

METHOD

1. Put the peach purée and sugar into the saucepan, heat gently until the sugar has dissolved, stirring all the time with the tablespoon, then boil for 5 minutes. Remove from the heat. Dissolve the gelatine in 2 tablespoons water in a basin over a pan of hot water.

2. Cut the jelly into pieces and mix with the boiled sugar and fruit purée. Stir until dissolved, then add the gelatine.

3. Pour the peach jelly into the tin, which should be lightly wetted, and leave for twenty-four hours until completely set, preferably in the refrigerator.

4. Cut the set jellies into squares or shapes and roll in caster sugar, then serve in paper sweet cases.

Liqueur Jellies

Makes approximately 1 ¼ lb (560 gm) jellies

EQUIPMENT

1 large heavy pan
1 metal tablespoon
1 sugar thermometer
1 small basin
1 tin 8 in (20 cm) square

INGREDIENTS

Imperial	Metric	Cup	Ingredient
1 lb	450 gm	2	**Granulated sugar**
¼ pt	150 ml	⅔	**Water**
2 tablespoons	–	–	**Powdered gelatine**
To taste	–	–	**Liqueur and colouring**

METHOD

1. Put the sugar and water into the saucepan and heat gently, stirring all the time with the tablespoon until the sugar has dissolved completely.

2. Bring to the boil and boil until the temperature reaches 240°F / 116°C.

3. Meanwhile, dissolve the gelatine with a little water in the small basin standing in a pan of hot water, then add this to the boiled syrup together with the liqueur and colouring. (About 1 tablespoon liqueur will be sufficient for this quantity of syrup).

4. Pour the jelly syrup into the tin, which should be slightly wetted, then allow to set for twenty-four hours.

5. Cut the jellies into cubes or fancy shapes, roll them in caster sugar and place in small fluted sweet cases.

Turkish Delight

Makes approximately 1 ¼ lb (560 gm) Turkish Delight

EQUIPMENT

1 medium saucepan
1 metal tablespoon
1 shallow tin, 8 in x 6 in (20 cm x 15 cm) square
1 sharp knife

INGREDIENTS

Imperial	Metric	Cup	Ingredient
½ pt	300 ml	1 ¼	**Hot water**
3 level tablespoons	–	–	**Powdered gelatine**
1 lb	450 gm	2	**Granulated sugar**
¼ level teaspoon	–	–	**Citric acid**
¼ level teaspoon	–	–	**Vanilla essence**
¼ level teaspoon	–	–	**Almond essence**
¼ level teaspoon	–	–	**Red colouring**
2 oz	56 gm	⅓	**Icing sugar**
2 tablespoons	–	–	**Cornflour**

METHOD

1. Put the hot water into the saucepan and sprinkle the gelatine over it. Add the sugar and citric acid. Heat over a gentle heat, stirring all the time, until the sugar has completely dissolved.

2. Bring the syrup to the boil and boil for 20 minutes. Remove from heat. Leave to stand for about 10 minutes without stirring, then add the vanilla and almond essences.

3. Put half the mixture into the tin. Colour

Left: Turkish Delight   *Above: Turkish Delight and jellies*   *Below: Fruit jellies*

the other half with the red colouring and pour it over the natural-coloured layer. Leave to set for twenty-four hours in a cool place.

4. Lay a sheet of greaseproof paper on the work surface. Sift the cornflour and icing sugar evenly over the paper.

5. Unmould the Turkish Delight and turn onto the paper. Cut into even squares with the sharp knife. Toss in extra sifted cornflour and then pack in greaseproof paper and store in an airtight tin or box.

Greek Turkish Delight

1. Follow recipe and method for Turkish Delight, omitting flavourings and colouring.
2. Flavour the syrup with a few drops of rosewater.
3. Add 3 tablespoons chopped, browned almonds before putting the mixture into the tin.

Peppermint Turkish Delight

1. Follow recipe and method for Turkish Delight, omitting flavourings and colouring.
2. Add 3-4 drops peppermint essence and a little green food colouring after the gelatine syrup has stood for 10 minutes.

9. Boiled Sweets

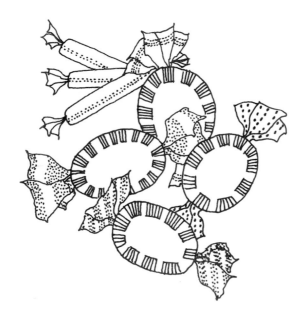

The syrup for boiled sweets is boiled until the 'hard crack' stage (see page 10) and should not be disturbed once the sugar has dissolved. It can be flavoured and coloured to give a wide variety of sweets which can be snipped and twisted when the candy is cool enough to handle.

Orange and Lemon Drops

Makes approximately 1 ½ lb (675 gm) fruit drops

EQUIPMENT

1 large heavy pan
2 lightly greased tins 6 in (15 cm) square
1 sugar thermometer

INGREDIENTS

Imperial	Metric	Cup	Ingredient
1 lb	450 gm	2	**Granulated sugar**
4 oz	112 gm	⅔	**Glucose**
6 fl oz	180 gm	¾	**Water**
1 teaspoon	–	–	**Cream of tartar**
½ teaspoon	–	–	**Lemon essence**
½ teaspoon	–	–	**Orange essence**

METHOD

1. Dissolve the sugar and glucose in the water over a low heat, then bring the mixture to the boil and boil until the temperature reaches 310°F / 154°C.
2. Add cream of tartar and pour the syrup into the two greased tins and colour one half orange and flavour it with the orange essence. Add the lemon essence to the other half and colour it with yellow colouring.
3. As soon as the mixture is cool enough to handle, roll it up, then cut small pieces from the mass and roll them into balls. Dip in icing sugar and then wrap in twists of cellophane paper.

Clear Mints

1. Follow recipe and method for Orange and Lemon Drops, omitting the fruit essences and adding ½ teaspoon peppermint essence.
2. Pour the boiled syrup into a greased 8 in (20 cm) square tin.
3. Cool until manageable, roll up and then snip off pieces about ½ in (1 ¼ cm) square, using oiled scissors. Wrap in twists of clear cellophane paper.

Acid Drops

Makes approximately 1 lb (450 gm) acid drops

EQUIPMENT

1 large heavy pan
1 metal tablespoon
1 well greased baking sheet
1 sugar thermometer
1 teaspoon

INGREDIENTS

Imperial	Metric	Cup	Ingredient
1 lb	*450 gm*	*2*	**Granulated sugar**
¼ teaspoon	*–*	*–*	**Cream of tartar**
4 fl oz	*120 ml*	*½*	**Water**
Few drops	*–*	*–*	**Lemon essence**
1 small teaspoon	*–*	*–*	**Tartaric acid**

METHOD

1. Put the sugar, cream of tartar and water into the saucepan, and heat gently until the sugar has dissolved, stirring all the time with the tablespoon.

2. Bring to the boil, and cook, without stirring, until the temperature reaches 310°F / 154°C.

3. Remove from the heat, dissolve the tartaric acid in a little warm water and add to the cooked syrup.

4. Leave syrup to cool slightly and begin to thicken, then using a teaspoon, and oiling it regularly form round drops on the oiled baking sheet and allow to cool and set completely before removing and wrapping in cellophane paper. Pack in tins or jars.

Old-fashioned Mint Humbugs

Makes approximately 1 lb (450 gm) humbugs

EQUIPMENT

1 large heavy pan
1 metal tablespoon
1 sugar thermometer
2 small shallow greased tins

INGREDIENTS

Imperial	Metric	Cup	Ingredient
1 lb	*450 gm*	*2*	**Granulated sugar**
¼ level teaspoon	*–*	*–*	**Cream of tartar**
¼ pt	*150 ml*	*⅔*	**Water**
½	*–*	*–*	**Lemon, juice**
1 teaspoon	*–*	*–*	**Peppermint essence**
Few drops	*–*	*–*	**Brown colouring**

METHOD

1. Put the sugar, cream of tartar and water into the saucepan and heat gently, stirring all the time with the tablespoon, until the sugar has dissolved.

2. Bring to the boil and cook without stirring until the temperature reaches 310°F / 154°C and remove from the heat.

3. Strain the lemon juice into the syrup and then boil again until the temperature returns to 310°F / 154°C.

4. Add the peppermint essence. Pour half the mixture into one prepared tin. Add colouring to the remaining syrup, then pour into the other tin.

5. As soon as the mixture is cool enough to handle, roll the sides to the centre and pull, fold back and pull again until it becomes semi-opaque. Repeat the process with the brown coloured candy.

6. Roll each piece into a thin roll, then twist the two colours together before cutting in suitably sized pieces with oiled scissors and wrapping in cellophane paper.

Barley Sugar Sticks

Makes approximately 1 lb (450 gm) sticks

EQUIPMENT

1 large heavy saucepan
1 metal tablespoon
1 sugar thermometer
1 lightly greased baking sheet
Scissors

INGREDIENTS

Imperial	Metric	Cup	Ingredient
1 lb	*450 gm*	*2*	**Granulated sugar**
¼ pt	*300 ml*	*⅔*	**Water**
Good pinch	*–*	*–*	**Cream of tartar**
½	*–*	*–*	**Lemon, juice**

METHOD

1. Put sugar and water into the saucepan and heat gently until the sugar has dissolved then stir in the cream of tartar.

2. Bring to the boil and cook until the thermometer registers 240°F / 116°C, then add the prepared lemon juice.

3. Boil to 310°F / 154°C and pour onto the prepared baking sheet.

4. Cool slightly and when firm enough to handle cut into strips with well oiled scissors. Twist these strips carefully in opposite directions then place on waxed paper and leave until completely set.

Note:
■ *Barley sugar sticks can be wrapped in cellophane and then stored in jars until required.*

Right: Orange and lemon boiled sweets, clear mints and acid drops

Left: Humbugs, barley sugars and clear mints

10. Candied Fruits

Candying fruits is merely a way of preserving fruits by using a sugar syrup. Essentially it is a process whereby the fruit is soaked in a syrup, which has more sugar added each day over a period of time, until the fruit is completely impregnated with sugar.

The most suitable fruits are those which have a positive flavour and a firm texture (e.g. pears, pineapple, apricots, oranges, cherries). The fruits can be fresh or canned, but should not be soaked in the same syrup. Always choose ripe but firm and unblemished fruits. Those which have the skins left on, such as apricots or plums, must be pricked all over with a fork to allow the sugar to soak into the fruit. Larger fruits, such as peaches and pears, should be peeled and cut into halves or quarters. Add a squeeze of lemon juice to pears and apples to help prevent discoloration.

Cook the prepared fruits in just enough boiling water to cover them, and when they are just tender but still retain their perfect shape, they will be ready to candy. Canned fruits need not be cooked, but they should be of a high quality.

Candied Fresh Fruits

For 1 lb (450 gm) prepared fruit

EQUIPMENT

1 heavy saucepan
1 metal tablespoon
1 large bowl

INGREDIENTS

Imperial	Metric	Cup	Ingredient
½ pt	300 ml	1 ¼	**Cooking water from fruit**
1 ½ lb	675 gm	3	**Sugar**
1 lb	450 gm	–	**Prepared fruit**

METHOD

1. Place the water and 6 oz (170 gm / ¾ cup) sugar in a saucepan and heat until the sugar dissolves, stirring all the time with the metal tablespoon. Bring to the boil and pour over the fruit. Leave to soak for twenty-four hours.

2. On the second day, drain off the syrup, add 2 oz (56 gm / ¼ cup) sugar, dissolve, bring to the boil and pour over the fruit. Soak for twenty-four hours.

Right: crystallized fruits

122

3. Repeat the process for 5 more days, then on the sixth day add 3 oz (80 gm / ⅓ cup) sugar to the strained syrup, dissolve and soak for forty-eight hours.
4. After forty-eight hours repeat the process with 3 oz (80 gm / ⅓ cup) sugar and leave it for 4 days.
5. To finish the fruits, cover lightly and leave in a warm place for 2 or 3 days until completely dry, turning 2 or 3 times (or see below).

■*Note. The fruits must be soaked for the full time be-*

fore the next process is carried out. If the amount of syrup is insufficient to cover the fruit, make more of the same strength and increase the amounts of sugar in the same proportions, i.e.

¾ pt	*450 ml*	*2 cups*	**Fruit juice**
9 oz	*250 ml*	*1 + cup*	**Sugar**

and then add 3 oz (90 gm / ⅓ cup) sugar on the second day, and on the sixth day add 4½ oz (127 gm / ½ + cups) sugar.
   When the fruits are thoroughly dry, pack in cardboard or wooden boxes with layers of waxed paper in between.

Finishing the Fruits

Crystallizing
Dip each piece of fruit quickly into boiling water and roll in caster sugar.

Glacé
To glacé the fruits, prepare a fresh syrup with 1 lb (450 gm / 2 cups) sugar and ¼ pt (150 ml / ⅔ cup) water and boil for 1 minute. Put the syrup into a basin in a pan of boiling water and cover with a cloth. Ladle a little syrup into a cup, dip the fruit in boiling water for about 20 seconds, then dip into the syrup one at a time. Place the glacéed fruits onto a wire rack to dry.

Note:
■ *The syrup in the cup should be replaced with fresh syrup from the basin as it becomes dull.*

Marrons Glacés

Makes approximately 2 lb (900 gm) marrons

EQUIPMENT

1 large heavy pan
1 metal tablespoon
1 screw-top bottling jar

INGREDIENTS

Imperial	Metric	Cup	Ingredient
8 oz	*225 gm*	*1*	**Granulated sugar**
8 oz	*225 gm*	*1 ¼*	**Glucose**
6 fl oz	*180 ml*	*¾*	**Water**
12 oz	*340 gm*	*–*	**Canned chestnuts**
Few drops	*–*	*–*	**Vanilla essence**

METHOD

1. Put the sugar, glucose and water into a saucepan large enough to hold the sugar and the chestnuts, then heat gently until the sugars are dissolved, stirring all the time with the tablespoon.

2. Bring the syrup to the boil, remove from the heat, add the chestnuts and bring back to the boil.
3. Remove the pan from the heat, cover and allow to stand overnight.

124

4. On the second day reboil the chestnuts and the syrup in the pan, remove from the heat, cover and leave for another night.
5. On the third day add about 6 drops of vanilla essence, and bring to the boil.
6. Warm the bottling jars in the oven, fill with the chestnuts and then cover with syrup. Seal and store in a cool place.

Note:
■ When the chestnuts are required they can be served straight from the bottle, or drained and wrapped in small pieces of coloured aluminium foil and twists of cellophane paper. Once they have been removed from the jar, they should be consumed within a day or two.

11. Caramels

Caramels and fudges could be confused, as the cooking temperatures are very similar. The basic difference is that caramels are *not* beaten and syrup does not 'grain' (see page 192). The texture is therefore smooth and velvety. If the syrup is boiled to, say, 245°F / 118°C, the caramels will be fairly soft – the higher the temperature the firmer the caramels. Just as jelly desserts need more gelatine in hot weather, so the sugar syrup for caramels should be boiled to a slightly higher temperature to prevent them from becoming too sticky.

The best caramels are made with cream, but a more economical method is to substitute milk and butter in the proportion of 1 tablespoon butter to 8 fl.oz milk. There are several points which should be borne in mind when making a batch of caramels:

a Use a large thick saucepan, as the mixture boils up very fast. Place an asbestos mat between hotplate and saucepan to prevent mixture from burning.

b A little glucose must be added, and the mixture should be stirred gently during the cooking time. While the syrup is dissolving stir it gently with a wooden spoon. While it is boiling, stir it with the thermometer. This will prevent the caramel from sticking to the bulb of the thermometer, causing it to register falsely. The glucose will soften the mixture and prevent it from graining (see page 192). But take care to follow the recipe accurately, for if too much glucose is added the caramels will not set firmly.

c When the syrup is within 10° or 15°F of the final temperature, lower the heat a little to prevent it from overheating and burning.

d As soon as the syrup has reached the required temperature, remove the pan from the heat immediately and pour quickly into an oiled tin. The syrup retains the heat and will continue cooking even after the pan has left the cooker.

e Don't scrape the pan out onto the mass of poured-out caramel, as the scrapings may crystallize and cause the whole batch to turn sugary.

f Cutting the cooled caramel needs some care. The best method is to remove the mass from the tin with a broad-bladed knife and lay it on a board. Carefully wipe the surface of the caramel with kitchen paper to remove any oil. Cut into suitably sized pieces with a large sharp knife. Do not allow the caramels to touch once they have been cut, as they will stick together. Wrap in *waxed* paper and store in an airtight tin in a cool, dry place.

g If possible store the caramels for 2 days before eating, as they become mellow and the flavour improves.

h If you have difficulty in obtaining the 6 in tins required for some of these recipes, use foil freezer trays of a comparable size.

Note:
■ *Caramels can, of course, be dipped in chocolate (see page 151) but they make a nice simple addition to a box of home-made chocolates when simply left plain and wrapped in thin waxed paper.*

Right: Cream caramels, satin caramels, Russian and blue ribbon caramels

Cream Caramels

Makes 1 lb (450 gm) caramels

EQUIPMENT

1 large heavy saucepan
1 wooden spoon
1 sugar thermometer
1 well greased tin, 6 in (15 cm) square
1 broad-bladed knife
1 large sharp knife

INGREDIENTS

Imperial	Metric	Cup	Ingredient
6 oz	170 gm	¾	**Granulated sugar**
4 tablespoons	–	–	**Milk**
1 tablespoon	–	–	**Glucose**
4 oz	112 gm	½	**Butter**
4 tablespoons	–	–	**Thin cream (warmed – see note below)**
2 teaspoons	–	–	**Vanilla essence**

METHOD

1. Put the sugar, milk, glucose and ⅓ of the butter into the saucepan. Melt slowly, stirring all the time.

2. As soon as all the ingredients are dissolved, bring briskly to the boil and add the second ⅓ of the butter. Continue stirring.

3. When the thermometer registers 235°F / 113°C, remove the pan from the heat.

4. Quickly add the last piece of butter, the warmed cream and the vanilla essence.

5. Return the pan to the heat and boil again to 250°F / 121°C. Pour immediately into the prepared tin. Leave to cool and set.

6. Remove the mass of caramel from the tin with a broad-bladed knife. Lay on a suitable work surface (e.g. a strong wooden board) and cut with a large sharp knife (see page 128). Wrap in plain waxed paper and store in an airtight tin in a cool, dry place.

Note:
■ When using cream, warm it slightly to prevent it from curdling in the mixture.

Nut Cream Caramels

1. Follow recipe and method for Cream Caramels.

2. Warm 1 tablespoon finely chopped nuts and arrange them in the prepared tin before the caramel is poured over.

Coconut Cream Caramels

1. Follow recipe and method for Cream Caramels.

2. Add 2 oz (56 gm / ¾ cup) desiccated coconut with the vanilla essence.

Rich Vanilla Caramels

Makes approximately 1¼ lb (560 gm) caramels

EQUIPMENT

1 large heavy based saucepan

1 wooden spoon
1 sugar thermometer
1 well greased shallow tin, about 7 in (18 cm) square
1 broad-bladed knife
1 large sharp knife

INGREDIENTS

Imperial	Metric	Cup	Ingredient
4 tablespoons	–	–	**Thin cream**
6 tablespoons	–	–	**Evaporated milk**
14 oz	*395 gm*	*1 ¾*	**Granulated sugar**
1 tablespoon	–	–	**Glucose**
Pinch	–	–	**Salt**
2 tablespoons	–	–	**Golden syrup**
1 oz	*30 gm*	*2 tablespoons*	**Butter**
1 teaspoon	–	–	**Vanilla essence**

METHOD

1. Put the cream, evaporated milk, sugar, glucose, salt, syrup and butter into the pan and heat gently until dissolved, stirring frequently.
2. Bring to the boil and boil to 255°F / 124°C stirring occasionally.
3. Remove from heat, beat in the vanilla essence and pour into the prepared tin.
4. Allow to become cold and set then remove from the tin and cut as for Cream Caramels. Wrap in thin waxed paper or cover in chocolate.

Russian Caramels

Makes approximately 1 ¼ lb (560 gm) caramels

EQUIPMENT

1 large heavy based saucepan
1 wooden spoon
1 sugar thermometer
1 well greased shallow tin, 7 in (18 cm) square
1 broad-bladed knife
1 large sharp knife

INGREDIENTS

Imperial	Metric	Cup	Ingredient
1 ½ oz	*45 gm*	*3 tablespoons*	**Butter**
¼ pt	*150 ml*	*⅔*	**Sweetened condensed milk**
8 oz	*225 gm*	*1*	**Granulated sugar**
¼ pt	*150 ml*	*⅔*	**Golden syrup**
1 tablespoon	–	–	**Glucose**
1 teaspoon	–	–	**Vanilla essence**

METHOD

1. Melt butter gently in the pan. Add condensed milk, sugar, syrup, and glucose, mixing well.
2. Dissolve ingredients over a low heat, stirring continuously.
3. Bring to the boil and boil to 255°F / 124°C stirring occasionally to prevent burning.
4. Remove from heat, beat in essence and pour into a prepared tin. Allow to set.
5. Cut and wrap as for Cream Caramels.

Russian Nut Caramels

1. Follow recipe and method for Russian Caramels.
2. Warm 2 tablespoons chopped nuts and arrange in the prepared tin before pouring on the caramel.

Chocolate Russian Caramels

1. Follow recipe and method for Russian Caramels.
2. Add 2 oz (56 gm) grated dessert chocolate when the caramel mixture has reached a temperature of 230°F / 110°C and continue to 255°F / 124°C.

Hard Caramels

Makes approximately 12 oz (340 gm) caramels

EQUIPMENT

1 large heavy saucepan
1 wooden spoon
1 sugar thermometer
1 broad-bladed knife
1 large sharp knife
1 well greased tin, 6 in (15 cm) square

INGREDIENTS

Imperial	Metric	Cup	Ingredient
8 oz	*225 gm*	*1*	***Granulated sugar***
2 level tablespoons	*–*	*–*	***Glucose***
1 tablespoon	*–*	*–*	***Golden syrup***
4 tablespoons	*–*	*–*	***Water***
4 tablespoons	*–*	*–*	***Milk***
Few drops	*–*	*–*	***Vanilla essence***

METHOD

1. Put all the ingredients, except for the vanilla essence, into the saucepan. Heat gently, stirring all the time, until the sugar has dissolved.
2. Bring to the boil, then heat slowly until the temperature reaches 255°F / 124°C. The mixture should be stirred occasionally during the cooking.
3. When the required temperature has been reached, add the vanilla essence. Pour the mixture quickly into the prepared tin.
4. When cold and set, remove from the tin and finish as for Cream Caramels.

Left: Hard caramels, golden honey caramels and coffee caramels

133

Coffee Caramels

1.　Follow recipe and method for Hard Caramels omitting the vanilla essence.

2.　Add 2 teaspoons coffee essence when the temperature has reached 245°F / 118°C then carry on heating to 255°F / 124°C.

Golden Honey Caramels

Makes approximately 8 oz (225 gm) caramels

EQUIPMENT

1 large heavy saucepan
1 sugar thermometer
1 well greased shallow tin, 6 in (15 cm) square
1 broad-bladed knife
1 large sharp knife
1 wooden spoon

INGREDIENTS

Imperial	Metric	Cup	Ingredient
8 tablespoons	–	–	**Clear honey**
4 tablespoons	–	–	**Thin cream**
3 oz	80 gm	½	**Demerara sugar**
1 tablespoon	–	–	**Glucose**
1 oz	30 gm	2 tablespoons	**Butter**
1 teaspoon	–	–	**Vanilla essence**

METHOD

1.　Put all the ingredients, except for the vanilla essence, into a large pan. Heat slowly until dissolved, stirring gently all the time.
2.　Bring the mixture to the boil, continuing to stir. Cook over a moderate heat until the temperature reaches 265°F / 129°C. Remove from the heat and add the vanilla essence. Pour immediately into the prepared tin, cool and finish as for Cream Caramels.

Caramel Crunchies

Makes approximately 1 lb (450 gm) crunchies

EQUIPMENT

1 large mixing bowl
1 large heavy saucepan
1 wooden spoon
1 well greased 2 lb loaf tin
1 sharp knife

INGREDIENTS

Imperial	Metric	Cup	Ingredient
2 oz	56 gm	2	**Cornflakes**
1 oz	30 gm	1	**Crispy rice cereal**
2 oz	56 gm	–	**Chocolate polka dots**
4 oz	112 gm	1	**Chopped walnuts**
8 tablespoons	–	¾	**Golden syrup**
2 oz	56 gm	¼	**Granulated sugar**
1 oz	30 gm	2 tablespoons	**Butter**
½ teaspoon	–	–	**Vanilla essence**

METHOD

1. Put the cereals, the chocolate and chopped walnuts into a large mixing bowl.
2. Put the golden syrup, sugar and butter in the saucepan and heat gently until the sugar has dissolved.
3. Bring to the boil, stirring constantly, and then boil for exactly 3 minutes.
4. Remove from the heat and cool for 10 minutes. Add the vanilla essence.
5. Beat the mixture with the wooden spoon until it turns light brown and thickens. Pour it quickly over the cereal mixture and toss until evenly distributed.
6. Spoon the mixture into the prepared tin and chill in the refrigerator for 1 to 2 hours until it is set. To serve, remove from the tin, dipping it in a basin of hot water to loosen the block if necessary, and cut into pieces.

Notes:
■ *The Caramel Crunchy does not need to be kept in the refrigerator once it is set. Cut into pieces or slices and wrap in plain waxed paper or, if it is to be eaten immediately, arrange in a small dish.*
■■ *The mixture can also be shaped with lightly greased hands or a spoon, if it is allowed to cool in the basin for 15 minutes after the caramel and cereals have been combined.*

Fruit and Nut Crunchies

1. Follow recipe and method for Caramel Crunchies, but omit the chocolate polka dots.
2. Add 3 oz (80 gm / ½ cup) seedless raisins.

Peanut Caramel Crunchies

1. Follow recipe and method for Caramel Crunchies, omitting the nuts.
2. Add 1 oz (30 gm / 1 cup) extra rice cereal and 3 tablespoons crunchy peanut butter.

Dipped Caramel Crunchies

1. Follow recipe and method for Caramel Crunchies.
2. Melt a little plain or milk chocolate in a small basin over a pan of hot water. Carefully dip each cut piece of Crunchy in the chocolate so that the base and a little of the sides is coated in the chocolate.
3. Shake them gently over the pan to remove excess chocolate, then place them on a sheet of waxed paper until the chocolate is set. Remove and store in a cool place.

Satin Caramels

Makes approximately 1 ¼ lb (560 gm) caramels

EQUIPMENT

1 large heavy based saucepan
1 metal tablespoon
1 wooden spoon
1 sugar thermometer
1 egg whisk or electric beater
1 well greased tin, 7 in (18 cm) square
1 sharp knife

INGREDIENTS

Imperial	Metric	Cup	Ingredient
4 fl.oz	120 ml	½	*Golden syrup*
4 fl.oz	120 ml	½	*Water*
1 lb	450 gm	2	*Granulated sugar*
1	–	–	*Egg white*
4 oz	112 gm	1	*Toasted chopped almonds*

METHOD

1. Put the syrup, water and sugar into the saucepan, heat gently until the sugar has dissolved, stirring continuously with the metal tablespoon, then bring to the boil and continue cooking without stirring until the temperature reaches 250°F / 121°C.

2. Just before the mixture reaches this temperature, beat the egg white until stiff but not dry.

3. Pour the caramel mixture over the egg white, whisking continually with an electric mixer or beating with a wooden spoon.

4. Continue beating until the mixture is thick and satiny, then stir in the nuts and shape the caramel into 4 loaves, 6 in x 1 ½ in (15 cm x 4 cm) and stand them on waxed paper. Cool until firm enough to cut into slices, but not cold and set hard, cool completely, then wrap the pieces in waxed paper.

Fruit and nut caramel sticks

Makes approximately 1 ¾ lb (785) caramel sticks

EQUIPMENT

1 small heavy saucepan
1 metal tablespoon
1 sugar thermometer
1 lightly greased tin, 8 in (20 cm) square

INGREDIENTS

Imperial	Metric	Cup	Ingredient
5 fl oz	150 ml	⅔	*Single cream*
4 fl oz	120 ml	½	*Golden syrup*
¾ teaspoon	–	–	*Salt*
3 oz	80 gm	½	*Dark soft brown sugar*
4 tablespoons	–	–	*Chopped walnuts*
8 oz	225 gm	1 ½	*Raisins*
¾ teaspoon	–	–	*Vanilla essence*

METHOD

1. Put the cream, syrup, salt and sugar into the saucepan and cook over a medium heat, stirring continuously until the sugar has dissolved.

2. Raise the heat a little and, still stirring occasionally to prevent the caramel from sticking, cook until the temperature reaches just below 255°F / 124°C. Remove from the heat.

3. Add the nuts, raisins and vanilla essence, then press into the prepared tin. Allow the caramel to cool and set overnight, then cut into about 44 very thin bars and wrap in waxed paper.

Above: Fruit and nut caramel sticks, peanut caramel crunchies, fruit and nut crunchie

Blue Ribbon Caramels

Makes approximately 1 ¾ lb (790 gm) caramels

EQUIPMENT

1 large heavy saucepan
1 metal tablespoon
1 sugar thermometer
1 wooden spoon
1 lightly greased tin, 9 in (22½ cm) square
1 large sharp knife

INGREDIENTS

Imperial	Metric	Cup	Ingredient
16 fl oz	480 ml	2	**Single cream**
Pinch	–	–	**Salt**
8 fl oz	240 ml	1	**Golden syrup**
1 lb	450 gm	2	**Granulated sugar**
8 fl oz	240 ml	1	**Evaporated milk**
4 oz	112 gm	–	**Grated plain chocolate**
1 ½ teaspoons	–	–	**Vanilla essence**

METHOD

1. Put 8 fl oz (240 ml / 1 cup) cream, the salt, syrup and sugar into the saucepan. Bring to the boil stirring continuously with the tablespoon, until all the sugar has completely dissolved.

2. Slowly add the remaining cream, still

137

stirring, and when the sugar thermometer registers 232°F / 111°C slowly add the evaporated milk, at the same time making sure the candy does not stop boiling.

3. Still stirring occasionally, add the grated chocolate and cook to 250°F / 121°C.

4. Remove the pan from the heat and add the vanilla essence. Pour into the prepared pan and allow to cool. As soon as the caramel is set, cut it into 1 in (2½ cm) squares and wrap in lightly waxed paper if not immediately required.

Nut Blue Ribbon Caramels

1. Follow recipe and method for Blue Ribbon Caramels.
2. Add 4 tablespoons chopped walnuts, almonds or hazelnuts with the vanilla essence.

Fruit Blue Ribbon Caramels

1. Follow recipe and method for Blue Ribbon Caramels.
2. Add 4 tablespoons dried fruit with the vanilla essence.

Brazil Blue Ribbon Caramels

1. Follow recipe and method for Blue Ribbon Caramels.

2. Place the caramel in a lightly greased Swiss roll tin, then cut into oblong pieces.
3. Wrap each piece around a whole shelled brazil nut. Wrap in lightly waxed paper.

Cashew Nut Snaps

1. Follow recipe and method for Blue Ribbon Caramels.
2. Arrange groups of 3 cashew nuts on a lightly greased baking sheet, leaving about 2 in (5 cm) in between each group of nuts.
3. Spoon 1 teaspoon of hot caramel over each group. Leave to cool a little, then press into a neat shape, letting parts of the nuts show through. Wrap in lightly waxed paper.

12. Truffles

Truffles are a delicious uncooked confection. They usually have a marzipan or cake crumb base and are flavoured with rum or sherry. Chopped dried fruits or nuts can be added to make interesting variations. The truffles are rolled in chocolate vermicelli or powdered drinking chocolate to give a characteristic finish.

Almond Truffles

Makes approximately 12 oz (340 gm) truffles

EQUIPMENT

1 large mixing bowl
1 small basin

INGREDIENTS

Imperial	Metric	Cup	Ingredient
4 oz	112 gm	1	**Ground almonds**
4 oz	112 gm	1 ¼	**Cake crumbs**
4 oz	112 gm	½	**Caster sugar**
A little	–	–	**Apricot jam**
2 tablespoons	–	–	**Sherry**

METHOD

1. Mix the almonds, cake crumbs and caster sugar in the mixing bowl, then add sufficient apricot jam and sherry to moisten the mixture so that when it is kneaded it is a fairly firm dough.
2. Mould small pieces of truffle into balls then toss them in the small basin, in chocolate vermicelli or powdered drinking chocolate.
3. Place in small fluted paper sweet cases to harden a little, then eat within four or five days.

Chocolate Truffles

Makes approximately 8 oz (225 gm) truffles

EQUIPMENT

1 saucepan

1 wooden spoon
2 small pudding basins

INGREDIENTS

Imperial	Metric	Cup	Ingredient
4 tablespoons	–	–	**Sweetened condensed milk**
1 tablespoon	–	–	**Cocoa powder**
1 oz	30 gm	2 table-spoons	**Butter**
4 oz	112 gm	1 ¼	**Cake crumbs**
2 tablespoons	–	–	**Seedless raisins**
A little	–	–	**Chocolate vermicelli**
A little	–	–	**Drinking chocolate**

METHOD

1. Heat the milk, cocoa and butter in the saucepan, stirring until it is well blended.

2. Remove the pan from the heat and stir in sufficient cake crumbs to make a stiff, manageable mixture, then add the raisins.

3. Mould pieces of truffle into small marble sized balls, then put the vermicelli and the drinking chocolate powder into the two small basins and toss half the balls in vermicelli and the other half in chocolate powder. Place the truffles in small fluted paper sweet cases and refrigerate until required.

Note:
■ *These should be eaten within a few days of being made.*

French Coffee Truffles

Makes approximately 12 oz (340 gm) truffles

EQUIPMENT

1 medium sized mixing bowl
1 small pudding basin
1 wooden spoon

INGREDIENTS

Imperial	Metric	Cup	Ingredient
6 oz	170 gm	1	**Sifted icing sugar**
1	–	–	**Egg yolk**
1 small teaspoon	–	–	**Instant coffee dissolved in a little hot water**
4 oz	112 gm	½	**Unsalted butter**
A little	–	–	**Drinking chocolate powder**

METHOD

1. Beat the sugar, egg yolk and dissolved coffee together in the mixing bowl. Gradually beat in the butter until the mixture resembles a thick paste.

2. Mould into small marble sized balls, then toss in the drinking chocolate in the small pudding basin. Serve very fresh in fluted paper sweet cases. Store for 2 or 3 days in the refrigerator if required.

Cream Truffles

Makes approximately 16 truffles

EQUIPMENT

2 small pudding basins
1 large saucepan
1 wooden spoon
1 metal tablespoon

INGREDIENTS

Imperial	Metric	Cup	Ingredient
2 oz	56 gm	–	**Dessert chocolate**
2 tablespoons	–	–	**Thin cream**
Few drops	–	–	**Vanilla essence**
8 oz	225 gm	1 ½	**Sifted icing sugar**
A little	–	–	**Drinking chocolate or chocolate vermicelli**

METHOD

1. Stand the pudding basin in a saucepan of hot water, with the water coming half way up the sides of the basin.
2. Break or cut the chocolate into small pieces and put it into the basin. Stir gently until completely melted, then beat until smooth with the wooden spoon.
3. Beat in the cream, 2 or 3 drops of vanilla essence and the icing sugar, a little at a time, until the mixture is well blended.
4. When the truffle mix is cold and firm, divide into 16 equally sized pieces and make into small balls. Quickly toss the balls in chocolate powder or press the chocolate vermicelli into the truffles and leave in a cool place to become firm. Present them piled on a small sweet platter, or place in small fluted paper sweet cases.

Coconut Truffles

1. Follow recipe and method for Cream Truffles, using only 4 oz (112 gm / ¾ cup) icing sugar.
2. Add 2 oz (56 gm / ¾ cup) desiccated coconut.
3. Finish the truffles by either rolling in chocolate powder or in toasted desiccated coconut.

Orange Truffles

Makes 10 truffles

EQUIPMENT

1 grater
1 mixing bowl
1 wooden spoon
1 small pudding basin

Following pages:
Left: Preparation of truffles

Right: Assorted truffles

143

INGREDIENTS

Imperial	Metric	Cup	Ingredient
4 oz	112 gm	–	**Milk chocolate**
3 oz	80 gm	½	**Sifted icing sugar**
Grated rind	–	–	**One small orange**
A few drops	–	–	**Vanilla essence**
To mix			**Double cream**

METHOD

1. Grate the chocolate on the coarse side of the grater. Put it into the mixing bowl together with the sifted icing sugar and grated orange peel.

2. Mix well and add a few drops vanilla essence and enough double cream to make a very stiff paste.

3. Divide the mixture into 10 equally sized pieces, roll into balls and coat them with chocolate powder or chocolate vermicelli. Serve in tiny fluted paper sweet cases.

Fruit 'n Nut Truffles

Makes approximately 25 truffles

EQUIPMENT

Mincer
1 mixing bowl

INGREDIENTS

Imperial	Metric	Cup	Ingredient
12 oz	340 gm	2 ¼	**Mixed dried fruit**
4 oz	112 gm	⅔	**Blanched almonds**
A little	–	–	**Toasted coconut**

METHOD

1. Mince or finely chop the mixed dried fruit and put into the mixing bowl.

2. Chop the almonds, not too finely, and mix these with the minced fruit.

3. Squeeze the fruit and nuts into small balls, about the size of a marble, then toss them in toasted coconut. Serve in fluted paper sweet cases.

Crunchy Truffles

Makes approximately 20 truffles

EQUIPMENT

1 small pudding basin
1 pan of hot water
1 wooden spoon

INGREDIENTS

Imperial	Metric	Cup	Ingredient
1 oz	30 gm	–	**Milk chocolate**
4 oz	112 gm	–	**Almond paste (bought or** **home-made** - see page 56)
1 tablespoon	–	–	**Caramel (see note below)**
½ teaspoon	–	–	**Rum or sweet sherry**

METHOD

1.   Melt the chocolate in the pudding basin over a pan of hot water.

2.   Beat the almond paste into the melted chocolate and then stir in the crushed caramel and rum or sherry.

3.   Allow the mixture to cool until it is manageable, then mould into small marble sized balls and coat in drinking chocolate powder or chocolate vermicelli.

4.   Place each truffle in a paper sweet case and store in the refrigerator until required.

Note:

■ To make caramel, dissolve a small quantity of granulated sugar in an equal quantity of water, then boil rapidly until the syrup begins to turn light caramel in colour. Pour immediately into an oiled tin, allow to become cold and brittle, then crush with a rolling pin between two sheets of greaseproof paper, or in a strong polythene bag. Crushed caramel can quite easily be stored in a polythene bag in a cool place until it is required.

French Cream Truffles

Makes approximately 1 lb (450 gm) truffles

EQUIPMENT

1 double boiler or medium sized mixing bowl over a pan of hot water
1 wooden spoon
1 small saucepan
1 sugar thermometer
Electric mixer or hand whisk
1 teaspoon

INGREDIENTS

Imperial	Metric	Cup	Ingredient
12 oz	340 gm	–	**Milk chocolate**
2½ fl oz	75 ml	⅓	**Single cream**
½ teaspoon	–	–	**Vanilla essence**
A little	–	–	**Drinking chocolate or** **chocolate vermicelli**

METHOD

1.   Melt the chocolate in the double boiler or in the bowl over hot water. As soon as it is melted, beat until smooth with a wooden spoon.

2.   Meanwhile, put the cream into the saucepan, heat to boiling point, then remove immediately from the heat and allow the temperature to fall to 130°F / 54°C.

3.   At this point add the warm cream to the melted chocolate all at one time, beat until smooth, then remove from the double boiler or pan of hot water, add the vanilla and cool.

4. When cool, beat with an electric mixer or a hand whisk until the candy is light and fluffy. Place in the refrigerator and cool until firm.

5. Using a teaspoon as a measure, roll small balls of the truffle mixture in the hands, then roll each immediately in the Drinking chocolate powder or in chocolate vermicelli.

Note:
■ *For a more unusual flavour, add a little cinnamon to the drinking chocolate.*

13. Chocolate Work

Dipping Centres

Dipping is perhaps the most difficult part of chocolate making, and the professional chocolate makers of Europe have generally been dipping chocolates for years. The expert will dip all his centres by hand but, as this takes some time to master, it is better for the beginner to use a dipping fork (see page 10).

Ideally you should use at least 3 lb (1,350 gm) of chocolate, which should be either commercially made confectioner's chocolate or chocolate which is sold for coating cakes and making chocolate moulds, etc., but smaller amounts (e.g. ½ lb) can be used quite successfully. However, if these are difficult to obtain, dessert or milk bars can be used, but of course this is more expensive. The chocolate should be melted in a double boiler (see page 11) or in a deep basin over a pan of hot water. There are two important points to remember when melting chocolate:

a   Never let any water drop into the melted chocolate, as it will ruin the whole batch.

b   Heat the chocolate gently and do not allow the water under the pan or basin to boil, otherwise the chocolate will deteriorate.

The temperature of the room is also important. It should be around 60°F / 17°C and the temperature of the chocolate must be between 85°F – 87°F / 29°C – 30°C. One way of gauging the correct temperature is to test little dabs of chocolate on heavy waxed paper. The mass of chocolate must be stirred continuously while these are cooling, as the bottom layer in the pan may get thick.

The chocolate is ready for dipping when a dab dries on the paper and mists over in about a minute. If the chocolate becomes too cold for dipping, merely reheat the water in the pan or double boiler to soften it. It can be softened time and time again, but at no time allow it to overheat.

When you are ready to start dipping the centres, have a large sheet of heavy waxed paper by the side of the pan and a skewer for smoothing off the surface under the dipping fork. Drop the centre into the chocolate, push it gently under the surface with the fork, then lift it up at once. Slide it down to the front edge of the fork, so that it will slip off easily when required. Move the skewer gently under the fork to remove surplus chocolate and when no more liquid chocolate will drip off lower the point of the fork onto the waxed paper and allow the finished chocolate to slide off. Push it very gently for a fraction of an inch across the paper to seal the base.

To finish the chocolates, keep the tip of the fork touching the chocolate, then raise it, with a thread of chocolate attached, and make a pattern with the 'thread' on top of the chocolate. Alternatively, quickly dip the point of the fork into the pan of melted chocolate and then return it to the setting chocolate and make a pattern on top of the sweet. Always keep the same type of design on each type of centre so that they are easily identifiable.

Chocolates can quite easily be finished by decorating with a small piece of crystallized fruit or tiny cake decorations.

A simpler and cheaper method of covering chocolates is to place the centres on a wire cooling rack, allowing about 2 in (5 cm) in between each centre so that the sides will also be evenly coated with the chocolate. Stand the rack on aluminium foil or waxed paper so that the drips' can be taken off and re-melted for using a second time. Melt the chocolate as you would if you were dipping the chocolates, then spoon a little over each centre. Make a distinctive pattern on each type of centre by dipping a skewer in the melted chocolate and drawing the thread of chocolate across the setting sweets.

The only difference between these and the dipped chocolates is that the base will not be covered with chocolate, but they will taste just as delicious. Allow about 8 oz (225 gm) chocolate per 1 lb (450 gm) of centres.

Try not to handle the chocolates too much, otherwise the 'bloom' (see page 192) will be rubbed off. Place the finished chocolates into small paper sweet cases and then pack into tins or boxes with a sheet of waxed paper between each layer.

CHOCOLATE CENTRES

Nut Pâtés

Makes approximately 8 oz (225 gm) nut paté

EQUIPMENT

1 large mixing bowl
1 fork
1 rolling pin

INGREDIENTS

Imperial	Metric	Cup	Ingredient
4 oz	112 gm	1	**Ground nuts (almonds, hazelnuts, walnuts)**
4 oz	112 gm	½	**Caster sugar**
½	–	–	**Egg, lightly beaten**

METHOD

1. Put the ground nuts and caster sugar into the mixing bowl and then work half an egg into the mixture until all the ingredients are well blended.

2. Knead the dough lightly with the fingers until it is firm adding a little extra caster sugar if the dough is rather soft.

3. Colour as desired and roll out on a board dusted with icing sugar, then cut or shape as required.

Chocolate Nut Pâté

EQUIPMENT

1 large heavy saucepan
1 double boiler or pudding basin inside a pan of hot water
1 wooden spoon
1 rolling-pin

Right: In round box – coffee drops, raisin diamonds, coffee canache, dark hazelnuts, chocolate gingers, Valencias, chocolate cherries, almonds, Jamaicans, walnut squares and nut centres
In square box – Rembrandts, almond squares, nut clusters, canache and canache truffles, chocolate gingers, cherries and fruit and nut clusters

INGREDIENTS

Imperial	Metric	Cup	Ingredient
4 oz	112 gm	½	*Caster sugar*
2 tablespoons	–	–	*Water*
4 oz	112 gm	1	*Ground nuts*
4 oz	112 gm	–	*Plain or milk chocolate*

METHOD

1. Put the caster sugar and water in the saucepan and heat gently, stirring continuously, until the sugar has dissolved.
2. Bring to the boil and boil quickly for one minute.
3. Stir in the ground nuts and allow to cool while melting the chocolate by breaking it or cutting it into small pieces and placing it in a double boiler or in a pudding basin over a pan of hot water. Stir until melted.
4. Mix the chocolate with the cooled nut and syrup mixture. Blend together and allow to cool before rolling out and cutting into the required shapes.

SUGGESTIONS FOR COATING AND FLAVOURING NUT PÂTÉS.

All these suggestions are suitable for plain or chocolate nut pâtés, or the boiled marzipan recipe on page 56.

Almond Squares

1. Follow recipe and method for Nut Pâté.
2. Roll out to about ½ in (1 cm) thick and cut into 1 in (2½ cm) squares.
3. Dip or coat in milk chocolate and then drizzle (see note) a pattern on the top with dark chocolate and allow to set on waxed paper.

Note:
■ To 'drizzle' chocolate, make a small bag from greaseproof paper and fill with cooled melted chocolate. Snip the end from the bag and allow the chocolate to run out whilst moving the bag across the sweets.

Dark Hazelnut Circles

1. Follow recipe and method for Nut Pâté, using hazelnuts.
2. Roll out to about ½ in (1 cm) thick and cut into small 1 in / 2½ cm circles using a small plain pastry cutter.
3. Coat or dip in dark chocolate and garnish with a toasted hazelnut or chocolate coated nut (see page 159).
4. Allow to cool and set on waxed paper.

Walnut Squares

1. Follow recipe and method for Nut Pâté, using walnuts.
2. Roll out to about ½ in (1 cm) thick and cut into 1 in (2½ cm) squares.
3. Press half a walnut into the top, coat or dip in dark chocolate and allow to cool and set on waxed paper.

Jamaicans

1. Follow recipe and method for Nut Pâté, using almonds.
2. Flavour with rum or brandy essence.
3. Roll out ½ in (1 cm) thick and cut into small oblong shapes ½ in x 1 in (1¼ cm x 2½ cm).
4. Press 2 hazelnuts into the marzipan and dip or coat in dark chocolate. Allow to cool and set on waxed paper.

Coffee Drops

1. Follow recipe and method for Nut Pâté, using almonds.
2. Flavour with a little coffee essence.
3. Roll into marble sized balls, then make a small groove in the top with a skewer.
4. Dip or coat in plain or milk chocolate, and while the chocolate is still wet, sprinkle on a little chocolate vermicelli. Cool and set on waxed paper.

Raisin Diamonds

1. Follow recipe and method for Nut Pâté,

using almonds.

2. Colour with green colouring, add a few raisins and knead until the colour and dried fruit are evenly distributed.

3. Roll out ½ in (1 cm) thick and cut into diamond shapes.

4. Dip or coat in milk or plain chocolate and then make a pattern on the top by dipping the skewer in the chocolate, and drawing the 'thread' of chocolate on the skewer across the half set chocolate. Cool and set on waxed paper.

Chocolate Cherries

1. Follow recipe and method for Nut Pâté, using almonds.

2. Roll pâté very thinly and wrap around individual glacé or maraschino cherries.

3. Roll round in the hands to seal the pâté, then dip or coat in plain chocolate and cool and set on waxed paper.

Note:
■ If you are lucky enough to have a set of very small fancy cutters, all manner of shapes can be cut in plain or flavoured pâtés, dipped or coated in chocolate and then decorated with small silver balls, crystallized flowers or even a little piped icing.

Almond Roll

1. Follow recipe and method for Nut Pâté, using almonds.

2. Make a roll of the pâté and press chopped or split almonds along the length of it.

3. Place the roll on a wire rack and coat with plain chocolate. When completely set, cut into 1 in (2½ cm) pieces.

Chocolate Burrs

1. Follow recipe and method for Nut Pâté, using almonds. Flavour with grated orange peel and chopped candied peel. Roll into marble-sized balls.

2. Make more of the Nut Pâté, using hazelnuts and mix with finely crushed caramel (see page 147) and roll into marble sized balls.

3. To complete the chocolate burrs, melt milk or dessert chocolate in a basin over hot water, or a double boiler, and cool until thick but not set. Dip each ball into the chocolate, place on a wire mesh cooling rack and allow to cool until almost set. Then roll over the rack to make the chocolate coating rough in texture or roll in chocolate vermicelli. Lift onto waxed paper and leave to set.

Note:
■ Nut pâtés are attractive if coated in white chocolate by the method described for Chocolate Burrs.

Marzipan Pralines

1. Follow recipe and method for Chocolate Nut Pâté, using almonds.

2. Mix with a little crushed caramel (see note page 147) and roll out to about ½ in (1 cm) thick.

3. Cut into squares, coat in milk chocolate and allow to set on waxed paper. Drizzle (see note page 154) with plain chocolate.

Canache (Method 1)

Makes approximately 1¼ lb (560 gm) canache

EQUIPMENT

1 small heavy saucepan
1 wooden spoon
1 wire whisk

INGREDIENTS

Imperial	Metric	Cup	Ingredient
8 fl.oz	240 ml	1	*Single cream*
1 lb	450 gm	1 lb	*Grated plain chocolate*
1 oz	30 gm	2 tablespoons	*Butter*

METHOD

1. Put the cream into the saucepan and bring slowly to the boil, then add the grated chocolate.

2. Cook very gently, stirring all the time until the chocolate has melted, then whisk in the butter and continue whisking until the mixture is well blended

3. Cool and pipe when sufficiently cool to hold its shape.

Canache (Method 2)

Makes approximately 1 ¼ lb (560 gm) canache

EQUIPMENT

2 small pudding basins
1 pan of hot water
1 wire whisk
1 metal tablespoon

INGREDIENTS

Imperial	Metric	Cup	Ingredient
2 oz	56 gm	¼	*Caster sugar*
3	–	–	*Egg yolks*
8 fl.oz	240 ml	1	*Single cream*
1 lb	450 gm	–	*Chocolate*

METHOD

1. Mix together the sugar, egg yolks and cream. Beat well and cook in a pudding basin over hot water until the mixture thickens enough to coat the back of a tablespoon.

2. Melt the chocolate in the second pudding basin and mix the cooled custard with the chocolate.

3. Cool the canache until it will hold its shape when piped.

SHAPING CANACHE

Canache is really best suited to piping. Cool the finished mixture as described in the recipes, then pipe 1 in (2½ cm) rolls or circles onto waxed paper. Either a plain or star-shaped vegetable nozzle can be used to pipe the shapes. Refrigerate the canache centres until ready to be dipped or coated in chocolate. Dip in the usual way and garnish with a silver ball, a small piece of nut or crystallized flower.

Above: On stand – raisin and rum cups, coffee canache, orange, mocha, walnut, cherry and Madeira cups
In box and on plate – nut, fruit and nut and other assorted chocolates

---

Canache Truffles

1. Follow either recipe and method for Canache.
2. Pipe small 1 in (2½ cm) rolls onto waxed paper, allow to harden slightly, then roll in drinking chocolate powder, icing sugar or chopped nuts. Refrigerate until required.

Orange Canache

1. Follow either recipe and method for Canache.

2. Flavour with the finely grated peel of one orange and pipe or shape as required.

Rum Canache

1. Follow either recipe and method for Canache.
2. Flavour with a little rum essence and pipe or shape as required.

Brandy Canache

1. Follow either recipe and method for Canache.
2. Flavour with a little brandy essence and pipe or shape as required.

Coffee Canache

1. Follow either recipe and method for Canache.

2. Flavour with a little coffee essence and pipe or shape as required.

Nut Canache

1. Follow recipe and method for Canache.
2. Add 3 tablespoons finely chopped nuts and pipe or shape as required.

Rembrandt Chocolates

1. Follow recipe for Canache (method 2).
2. Add a few chopped toasted hazelnuts.
3. Pipe, using a plain vegetable nozzle, into round marble sized shapes on waxed paper and leave to set.
4. Cover with chocolate as for Chocolate Burrs (see page155).

Nut Clusters

Makes ½ lb (225 gm) clusters

EQUIPMENT

1 small pudding basin
1 pan of hot water
1 teaspoon
Waxed paper

INGREDIENTS

Imperial	Metric	Cup	Ingredient
4 oz	*112 gm*	–	**Plain or milk chocolate**
4 oz	*112 gm*	*good ½*	**Peanuts or broken walnuts**

METHOD

1. Break the chocolate into pieces and put it into the pudding basin.
2. Stand the pudding basin in the pan of hot water and stir gently until the chocolate has melted and become smooth and liquid.

3. Stir the nuts into the chocolate until they are all well coated in chocolate, then spoon small amounts onto waxed paper and leave to set.
4. Present in small fluted paper cups.

Fruit and Nut Clusters

1. Follow recipe and method for Nut Clusters but use only 2 oz (56 gm / 1 cup) broken nuts or peanuts.
2. Add 2 oz (56 gm / ½ cup) seedless raisins.

Half-Dipped Chocolate Gingers

1. Cut pieces of crystallized ginger in half, then half dip in dessert chocolate.
2. Leave until set on a sheet of waxed paper.

Candied Matchsticks

1. Cut candied orange or lemon peel into thin strips and dip in dessert chocolate.
2. Leave to dry on waxed paper.

Valencias

1. Follow recipe and method for Nut Pâté, using almonds.
2. Flavour with finely grated orange peel and roll out to about ½ in (1 cm) thick.
3. Cut into oblong shapes ½ in x 1 in (1¼ cm x.2½ cm) and coat in dessert chocolate. Leave to set on waxed paper.

4. While the chocolate is still a little wet, place two pieces of chocolate-covered candied fruit strips (see Candied Matchsticks above) along the length. Drizzle (see page 154) a little milk chocolate across each sweet.

Chocolate Nut Caramels

1. Follow recipe and method for Walnut Caramels (see page 130) but use a larger tin so that the caramels are thinner.
2. When set, cut into 1 in (2½ cm) squares and then place each square diagonally on a thin square of Chocolate Walnut Pâté (see page 152)
3. Coat in dessert or milk chocolate and allow to set on waxed paper.

Chocolate Dipped Nuts

1. Dip toasted almond halves or whole toasted hazelnuts in dessert chocolate.
2. Shake any excess chocolate from the nuts and roll in caster sugar.
3. Allow to set on waxed paper and then use to decorate chocolates.

Mint Thins

1. Follow recipe and method for Peppermint Fondant (see page 21).

2. Roll very thinly and cut into small squares.
3. Dip or coat in dessert chocolate and cool and dry on waxed paper.

Dutch Chocolate Creams

1. Follow recipe and method for Basic Centre Fondant (see page 15).
2. Soften the fondant and knead 4 oz (112 gm) melted chocolate into it.
3. Add 4 tablespoons of toasted ground almonds and 2 teaspoons tinted sugar crystals. Roll into small balls, allow to 'crust' (see page 192) and then dip or coat with milk or plain chocolate and set on waxed paper.

Chocolate Toasted Almonds

1. Dip lightly roasted whole almonds in dessert chocolate. Allow to set on waxed paper.
2. For a delicious addition to your box of chocolates, put two almonds together in fluted paper cups.

MAKING CHOCOLATE CUPS

Chocolate cups are delicious, attractive and very simple to make. The 'moulds' for the cups are made by using two paper sweet cases one inside the other.

Melt a little milk or dessert chocolate in a basin over hot water. Using a teaspoon, spoon a little melted chocolate into the paper cases, then work it up the sides of the cases, making sure that all the paper is covered. Allow to dry and set completely, then repeat the chocolate process if it seems a little thin. Keep the paper cases around the cups and then fill with one of the fillings mentioned below.

To finish the sweets, spoon a little melted chocolate over each filled cup and push to the edges so that the filling is completely sealed with chocolate. Store in a cool place and serve with the paper cases still on so that the chocolate does not melt when handled.

Cherry Madeira Cups

1. Crush a little stale sponge cake or some sponge fingers and moisten with enough madeira or sweet sherry to make a firm mass.
2. Put a layer of madeira sponge in the base of each cup, place half a canned, pitted cherry on top and fill the cup with madeira sponge.
3. Finish as described above.

Coffee Canache Cups

1. Follow recipe and method for Coffee Canache.
2. Spoon a little canache into each cup.
3. Finish as described above.

Orange Canache Cups

1. Follow recipe and method for Orange Canache (see page157).
2. Spoon a little canache into each cup.
3. Finish as described above.

Rum and Raisin Cups

1. Cover enough raisins to fill the cups with rum and soak for about 2 hours.
2. Spoon into the cups.
3. Finish as described above.

Mocha Cups

1. Beat 2 oz (56 gm) unsalted butter with 2 oz (56 gm / ⅓ cup) sifted icing sugar until the mixture is light and smooth.
2. Flavour with 2 teaspoons coffee essence and then, using a star-shaped nozzle, pipe a little coffee butter cream into prepared chocolate cups.
3. Decorate each finished cup with half a toasted almond.

Walnut Cups

1. Follow recipe and method for Chocolate Nut Pâté, using walnuts.
2. Using a star-shaped nozzle, pipe a little pâté into each prepared chocolate cup.
3. Finish as described above and top with a piece of walnut.

Note:
■ The following sweets can be used as chocolate centres:
Marshmallows, any flavour (see p 67)
Caramels, any flavour (see p.130)
Fudge, any flavour (see p.25)
Basic Centre Fondant (see p.15)
Plain toffee (see p.74)
Peppermint toffee (see p.75)
Butterscotch (see p.78)
Peanut Brittle (see p.78)
French Almond Brittle (see p.79)
Jellies, any flavour (see p.107)
Turkish delight (see p.109)
Plain or peppermint coconut Ice (see p.173)
Nougat – plain, chocolate, American or cashew (see p.99)

MAKING EASTER EGGS

Plastic moulds for making Easter eggs are sometimes available at confectionery houses or on special offer from chocolate manufacturers. However, if you are not able to actually make your own eggs, hollow, chocolate eggs bought from a shop can be decorated with coloured marzipan, small sweets or icing to make them more interesting and attractive.

How To Coat Easter Egg Moulds

Most moulds will have instructions but if not it is quite a simple process. Melt chocolate (plain or milk – but plain chocolate is easier to handle) in the top of a double saucepan or in a basin over hot water. Brush the inside of the mould with a thick layer of chocolate then chill until set. Repeat brushing thinly with chocolate and chilling three or four times until chocolate begins to come away from the edge of the mould. Carefully ease out chocolate shell. Stick two halves together with melted chocolate, chill until set, then decorate as desired.

Swinging Humpty

1. Join the two halves of a home-made egg

or, if you are using a bought egg, check that the two halves are in fact safely joined together. If they are not, brush a little melted chocolate around the edge of both halves and place carefully together. Leave until the chocolate is completely set.

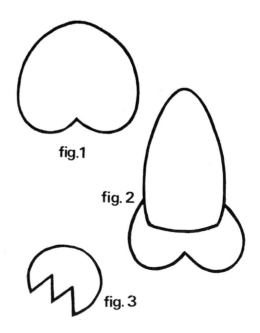

fig.1

fig. 2

fig. 3

2. Make a base by spooning a little melted milk or dessert chocolate onto a sheet of waxed paper and shaping it into a foot shape with the back of a teaspoon (see fig. 1).

3. While the chocolate is still wet, stand the wide end of the joined egg onto the back of the chocolate base so that the feet are protruding at the front (see Fig. 2). Support the upright egg with two food tins as props on either side of the egg until the base chocolate is firmly set.

4. To make the hair roll out yellow coloured marzipan very thinly on a surface dusted with icing sugar, then cut very thin strips, about 2 in (5 cm) long. Arrange the strips on top of the egg, overlapping them and curling them so that they resemble hair. Press the strips very lightly onto the chocolate to make them stick to the egg, taking care not to press too hard, or the egg will break.

5. Make the eyes from very thin jelly cake decorations, but if these are not available, make them by piping coloured icing onto the egg. Cut a light piece of jelly into a diamond shape to form the 'white' of the eye, and then cut a small circle of darker coloured sweet (use a very small round piping nozzle to do this) and stick it onto the white with a little melted chocolate. When the eyes are set, spread the back of the white with a little chocolate and stick it onto the face, just below the hair.

6. To make the mouth arrange small diamond shaped pieces of jelly sweet to make a mouth and stick these to the egg with dabs of melted chocolate. A pair of tweezers may be needed for this as it is quite a delicate operation. Alternatively, cut a piece of orange peel into a semi-circular mouth shape and then stick it onto the egg with a little melted chocolate.

7. To make the hands cut a pink marshmallow in half so that you have two thin circles of marshmallow. Use scissors as a knife will tend to pull and not cut. Take each circle and make two snips towards the centre (see Fig. 3) to make fingers then stick the hands onto the body, also with a dab of melted chocolate.

8. To make the toes roll small pieces of marzipan into tiny pill sized balls and stick 3 or 4 onto each foot.

Note:
■ This method can be adapted to make all sorts of appealing little characters from the basic egg shape.

Gloria Fish

1. For the body use a plain chocolate egg, without the traditional 'crazy paving' pattern on it. To make the scales, fins and tail, first draw the appropriate shapes on waxed paper (see Fig. 1) and then spoon a little melted plain or milk chocolate into the shape and spread it carefully to the edges. Smooth the chocolate with the back of a teaspoon and allow the shape to cool and set. You should make about 42 small scale shapes, one fin and one tail. When the fin and tail shapes are set, 'drizzle' (see page 154) with a little chocolate to make the markings.

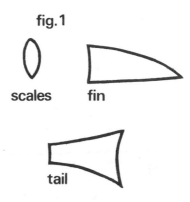

fig. 1

scales   fin

tail

2. To make the eyes and lips, cut 2½ in (1¼ cm) circles from very thinly rolled marzipan for the eyes and then 2 semi-circles 1 in (2½ cm) in diameter from slightly thicker rolled marzipan for the lips.

3. To assemble the fish, put a dab of melted chocolate onto the base of the egg and stick it onto a bought or home-made chocolate. Arrange the scales, overlapping each other, around the egg, attaching them with small dabs of chocolate. Stick the eyes, lips, fin and tail as shown in the diagram, and secure them in position with a little melted chocolate. Make the pupils of the eyes by sticking a small sweet onto the marzipan circles. Wrap the fish in clear cellophane paper and tie with a ribbon.

Following pages:
Right: Process of making Easter eggs

Left: Decorated Easter eggs

Grinning Toad

1. Use two halves of a large chocolate egg. Draw an egg shape on waxed paper, using the base of one half as a guide. Fill this shape in with melted chocolate and stand one half of the egg on it. Leave until completely set, then remove the egg and stand it on its curved surface. This forms the lower half of the head.

2. Colour a little marzipan with pink colouring and roll out two thin strips. Brush a little melted chocolate onto one side of each strip and stick one on the base edge of the other half of the egg which forms the top of the head, and one along the top edge of the base. Make a big marzipan tongue, also coloured pink, and fix this to the flat top of the head base. Carefully brush a little melted chocolate onto the rims of the two halves and stick them together so that the two halves are slightly open at the tongue end. Support them until they are set, then wrap in cellophane paper and tie with a narrow ribbon.

Bird House

1. Use a plain or patterned egg for the house. To make the base, roof and door, draw the shapes (see figs. 1, 2 and 3) onto waxed paper, in sizes proportional to the size of the egg. Flood the shapes with melted chocolate and allow it to set. When the roof shape is almost set, mark a square pattern on it, as shown in the picture, with a broad bladed knife.

2. Stick the broad end of the egg onto the base with melted chocolate and support it until it is completely set. Then, carefully stick the roof and door onto the egg with melted chocolate and again support it until set.

3. Make two small chickens (see fig. 4) out of marzipan and set one carefully on the door and the other on the base of the house. Use a silver ball for the eye and a piece of split almond as the beak. Decorate the roof with tiny crystallized flowers, sugar mushrooms, or small balls of marzipan half dipped in chocolate, resembling acorns.

Easter Basket

1. For this you need half a large chocolate egg and half a small chocolate egg. Stick the large chocolate half onto the small chocolate half back to back (Fig. 1) with melted chocolate.

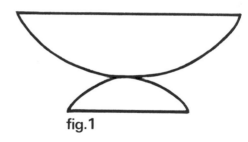

fig. 1

2. Decorate the edge of the large egg with toasted split almonds, sticking them on to the sides with a little melted chocolate.

3. When the two eggs are firmly stuck together, fill the large half with small foil-covered eggs, or a selection of home-made or bought chocolates. Wrap the completed egg in cellophane and tie with a ribbon.

Spring Chicken Egg

1. Use a plain or patterned chocolate egg. Make a base for the egg by drawing an oval shape 3 in x 2 in (7½ cm x 5 cm) onto waxed paper. Fill this in with a thick layer of chocolate. Stand the egg onto it and support it until it is completely set in position.

2. Select about 20 perfect walnut halves

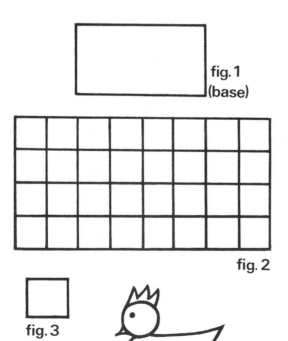

fig. 1
(base)

fig. 2

fig. 3

fig. 4

and position them around the join of the egg, sticking each with a little melted chocolate.

3. Mould two tiny chicken shapes (Fig. 1) from yellow marzipan, making the combs from

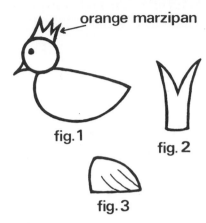

orange marzipan

fig. 1

fig. 2

fig. 3

orange marzipan and using two silver balls for the eyes. Draw a shape for the tail (Fig. 2) on waxed paper and fill in this shape with a little melted chocolate. Remove them from the waxed paper and attach them to the chickens with a dab of chocolate. Make small wing shapes (Fig. 3) and fix these onto the body with melted chocolate.

4. Stick the marzipan chickens onto the egg with melted chocolate. Wrap the completed egg in cellophane and tie with a ribbon.

Peter Penguin

1. Use a plain dark chocolate egg. Spread a little melted chocolate onto waxed paper and stand the wide end of the egg onto it. Support until set.

2. Make the feet by spooning a little dark chocolate onto waxed paper (see Fig. 1). When they are set, stick them onto the base of the egg with chocolate. Make the wings by drawing the shapes on waxed paper (Fig. 2) and then filling in with melted chocolate. When they are completely set, remove from the paper and stick halfway down the body with dabs of melted chocolate.

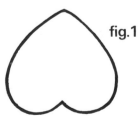

fig. 1

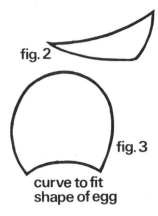

fig. 2

fig. 3

curve to fit shape of egg

3. Mould a head shape (Fig. 3) from marzipan, and then dip or coat it in dark chocolate. When this is completely set, stick it on top of the egg. Carefully stick two silver balls onto the head for eyes, and shape a beak out of yellow marzipan, then wrap the penguin in cellophane and tie with a plain ribbon.

Flower Egg

1. Use a plain or patterned chocolate egg. Mould 9 marzipan petals as shown in Fig. 1 and then make six slightly smaller ones for the middle of the flower. For the very centre of the flower, make four even smaller petals. You can use either yellow or pink marzipan for making the flower shape.

fig. 1

2. Carefully attach each petal to the egg with a dab of chocolate, building the flower up as shown in the picture.

3. To make the stamens in the centre, carefully press five small pieces of split, toasted almonds right in the centre of the middle petals.

4. Stick chocolate drops to the egg, with small dabs of melted chocolate, around the join of the egg. Wrap the completed egg in cellophane and tie with a ribbon.

14. Uncooked Sweets

These sweets are especially suitable for children to make because there is no danger from boiling syrups, hot saucepans etc. The younger sweetmakers may need help in melting chocolate, but apart from this the recipes have been kept as simple as possible.

Simple Basic (Uncooked) Fondant

Makes approximately 1 lb (450 gm) fondant

EQUIPMENT

1 large mixing bowl
1 sieve
1 fork
1 rolling-pin

INGREDIENTS

Imperial	Metric	Cup	Ingredient
4 tablespoons	–	–	**Evaporated milk**
1 lb	450 gm	3	**Icing sugar**

METHOD

1. Measure the evaporated milk into the mixing bowl, then sieve the icing sugar and gradually work it into the milk, using a fork, until all the sugar has been used.

2. Knead it with the hands until the fondant becomes smooth and easy to handle, then colour and mould into shapes.

Tangy Uncooked Fondant

1. Follow recipe and method for Simple Basic Fondant.
2. Add 4 tablespoons chopped candied peel before kneading.
3. Roll the fondant to about ½ in (1¼ cm) thick on a board lightly dusted with icing sugar, and cut into small shapes. Allow to harden a little.

Pineapple Uncooked Fondant

1. Follow recipe and method for Simple Basic Fondant.
2. Add 4 tablespoons chopped glacé pineapple before kneading.
3. Finish as for Tangy Uncooked Fondant.

Ginger Uncooked Fondant

1.   Follow recipe and method for Simple Basic Fondant.
2.   Add 4 tablespoons chopped crystallized ginger before kneading.
3.   Finish as for Tangy Uncooked Fondant.

Peppermint Creams

1.   Follow recipe and method for Simple Basic Fondant.
2.   Add a few drops oil of peppermint or peppermint essence. Roll out thinly and cut into small rounds using a small, plain pastry cutter.
3.   Lay on waxed paper and allow to set for about 5 hours. Put each sweet into a small fluted paper sweet case and store in an airtight tin.

Sugar Mice

1.   Follow recipe and method for Simple Basic Fondant.
2.   Shape pieces of fondant to resemble mice. Put currants for eyes and a thin piece of white string for a tail. These mice can be coloured pink with a few drops of cochineal, or left white.

Coffee Creams

1.   Follow recipe and method for Simple Basic Fondant.
2.   Flavour the fondant with a little coffee essence. Roll out thinly and cut into fancy shapes with small fluted pastry cutters.
3.   Decorate with a piece of walnut, or a lightly toasted hazelnut.

Chocolate Spirals

1.   Follow recipe and method for Simple Basic Fondant.
2.   Add 1 oz (30 gm) melted dessert chocolate to half the quantity of fondant, and knead until well blended.
3.   Roll the plain piece out thinly, using a little icing sugar to prevent the fondant from sticking, then roll the chocolate piece out to about the same size. Lay one piece on top of the other, trim the edges and roll up like a Swiss roll.
4.   Cut the roll into thin slices and lay each piece on waxed paper until it becomes firm enough to wrap in clear cellophane paper.

Cherry Fondants

1.   Follow recipe and method for Simple Basic Fondant
2.   Roll small pieces of unflavoured fondant into small balls, flatten slightly and then press half a glacé or maraschino cherry into the top of each one.
3.   Allow to harden for about 5 hours before eating.

Note:
■ As this type of fondant is not cooked, these sweets should be eaten within three days of making.

Nut and Raisin Fudge

Makes approximately 1 lb (450 gm) fudge

EQUIPMENT

1 large mixing bowl
1 sieve
1 pan of hot water
1 fork
1 lightly greased tin, 6 in (15 cm) square
1 palette knife

INGREDIENTS

Imperial	Metric	Cup	Ingredient
4 oz	112 gm	–	**Dessert chocolate**
½ oz	15 gm	1 tablespoon	**Butter**
2 tablespoons	–	–	**Evaporated milk**
8 oz	225 gm	1 ½	**Sifted icing sugar**
2 oz	56 gm	⅓	**Seedless raisins**
1 oz	30 gm	2 tablespoons	**Chopped salted peanuts**

METHOD

1. Put the mixing bowl over the pan of hot water and melt the chocolate. Add the butter and stir with the fork until the butter and chocolate are well blended, then remove from the heat and add the milk.

2. Work in the sifted icing sugar, a little at a time so that it becomes well mixed with the butter and chocolate mixture, then stir in the fruit and nuts.

3. Press the fudge into the lightly greased tin and smooth the top with a palette knife. Allow the fudge to become hard (this takes about 3 hours). Cut into squares and put each piece into a small fluted paper case or wrap in clear cellophane paper.

Chocolate Krispies

Makes approximately 8 oz (225 gm) krispies

EQUIPMENT

1 large mixing bowl
1 pan of hot water
1 lightly greased 7 in (18 cm) square tin
1 palette knife
1 sharp knife
1 metal tablespoon

INGREDIENTS

Imperial	Metric	Cup	Ingredient
4 oz	112 gm	–	**Dessert or milk chocolate**
3 oz	80 gm	3	**Cornflakes, lightly crushed**
2 tablespoons	–	–	**Seedless raisins**

METHOD

1. Stand the basin over the pan of hot water, break the chocolate into pieces and allow it to melt.

2. Stir in the crushed cornflakes and raisins and stir with the palette knife until both the flakes and raisins are well coated with chocolate.

3. Turn the mixture into the prepared tin and flatten with the knife.

4. Cool in the refrigerator, then cut into bars with the sharp knife.

Note:
■ *Chocolate Krispies should be eaten within a day of making, otherwise the flavour is spoilt. If you need to keep them for a few hours, they are best kept in the refrigerator to prevent the chocolate from melting.*

Right: Sugar mice, peppermint creams, chocolate spirals, nut and raisin fudge and chocolate krispies

170

Chocolate Chewing Nuts

Makes approximately 1 lb (450 gm) sweets

EQUIPMENT

1 large mixing bowl
1 sieve
1 wooden spoon
1 sharp knife

INGREDIENTS

Imperial	Metric	Cup	Ingredient
2 oz	56 gm	¼	**Butter**
2 tablespoons	–	–	**Golden syrup**
2 oz	56 gm	–	**Melted dessert chocolate**
3 drops	–	–	**Vanilla essence**
6 oz	170 gm	1	**Sifted icing sugar**
2 oz	56 gm	⅓ +	**Milk powder**

METHOD

1. Soften the butter, then mix it with the syrup in the mixing bowl until well blended.
2. Add the melted chocolate and the vanilla, then gradually mix in the sifted icing sugar and the milk powder.
3. Knead until all the ingredients are well combined, then mould into small balls. Toss the balls in a little extra icing sugar and allow to set on a sheet of waxed paper.

Note:
■ As an alternative, the mixture can be rolled into long rolls about ½ in (1 ¼ cm) round and then drizzled with liquid chocolate (see page 154) Leave until the chocolate is completely set and then cut the rolls diagonally into pieces. Lay each piece in a small fluted paper sweet case to serve.

Peppermint Chocolate Chewing Nuts

1. Follow recipe and method for Chocolate Chewing Nuts.
2. Add 3 drops oil of peppermint before kneading.
3. Finish as for Chocolate Chewing Nuts.

Caribbean Candies

Makes approximately 8 oz (225 gm) candies

EQUIPMENT

1 large mixing bowl
1 pan of hot water
1 fork
Small pattie tins
1 metal tablespoon
1 sharp knife

INGREDIENTS

Imperial	Metric	Cup	Ingredient
4 oz	112 gm	–	**Milk chocolate**
4 oz	112 gm	1 ¼	**Desiccated coconut**
10	–	–	**Glacé cherries**

METHOD

1. Put the mixing bowl over the pan of hot water. Break the chocolate into pieces, and place it in the warm basin.

2. When it has melted, stir in the coconut and cherries, cut into little pieces and mix until all the ingredients are well combined.

3. Press small amounts of candy into lightly greased pattie pans, or place small heaps on waxed paper then chill. Put each candy into a paper cup.

Note:
■ *These sweets are best left in the refrigerator until required. They should be eaten within three days of making.*

Honey Kusjes

Makes approximately 1 lb (450 gm) sweets

EQUIPMENT

1 large mixing bowl
1 fork
1 sharp knife

INGREDIENTS

Imperial	Metric	Cup	Ingredient
5 tablespoons	–	–	**Peanut butter (crunchy)**
4 tablespoons	–	–	**Clear honey**
4 oz	112 gm	¾	**Dried milk powder**
2 oz	56 gm	⅓	**Seedless raisins**
2 oz	56 gm	¼	**Chopped peanuts**

METHOD

1. Mix all the ingredients in a large mixing bowl, then knead lightly until a firm mass of candy is formed.

2. Press the candy into an oblong shape on waxed paper, about ½ in (1 ¼ cm) thick, then chill for three or four hours until firm. (This type of candy is always a little soft)

3. Cut into squares and put into small fluted paper cases to serve. Eat within four days of making.

Coconut Ice

Makes approximately 12 oz (340 gm) coconut ice

EQUIPMENT

1 large mixing bowl
1 rolling pin
1 sharp knife

Following pages:
Left: Coconut ice, fondant making, nut and raisin fudge
Above right: Cherry fondants, ginger fondants, tangy, pineapple fondants, white tangy fondants and coffee creams
Below right: Boxes of chocolate chewing nuts, honey kusjes, Caribbean candies, chocolate coated cherry fondants and chocolate treats

173

INGREDIENTS

Imperial	Metric	Cup	Ingredient
4 oz	112 gm	1 ½	*Desiccated coconut*
4 oz	112 gm	½	*Caster sugar*
Pinch	–	–	*Cream of tartar*
5 tablespoons	–	–	*Sweetened condensed milk*
A few drops	–	–	*Pink colouring*

METHOD

1. Mix the coconut, sugar and cream of tartar in the mixing bowl.
2. Work it together with the condensed milk so that a firm mass is formed, then colour one half with sufficient pink colouring to give a rose colour.
3. Roll out both halves using icing sugar to prevent sticking. Put one on top of the other, press lightly together, wrap in waxed paper and allow to set overnight, preferably in the refrigerator.
4. Cut into bars and store in an airtight tin or wrap in cellophane paper.

Chocolate-coated Cherry Fondant

Makes approximately 12 oz (340 gm) sweets

EQUIPMENT

1 egg whisk
1 wooden spoon
1 large mixing bowl
1 wire cooling rack
1 sharp knife

INGREDIENTS

Imperial	Metric	Cup	Ingredient
1	–	–	*Egg white*
8 oz	225 gm	1	*Caster sugar*
2 tablespoons	–	–	*Chopped cherries*
5 tablespoons	–	–	*Ground almonds*
1 tablespoon	–	–	*Grated lemon peel*
8 oz	225 gm	–	*Dessert chocolate*

METHOD

1. Beat the egg white until it is stiff, then beat in the sugar and the other ingredients.
2. Mould the fondant into narrow flat oblong shapes about 6 in long and wrap in waxed paper. Chill in the refrigerator.
3. Stand on a wire cooling rack over a sheet of waxed paper and cover with the chocolate, melted in a small basin over a pan of hot water. Leave to set in a cool place, cut into thin slices with a knife dipped in hot water and wrap in coloured aluminium foil, or set in fluted paper sweet cases.

Chocolate Treats

Makes approximately 18 treats

EQUIPMENT

Small paper sweet cases
1 small pudding basin over a pan of hot water
1 rolling-pin
1 wooden spoon
1 teaspoon

INGREDIENTS

Imperial	Metric	Cup	Ingredient
4 oz	112 gm	–	**Plain or milk chocolate**
6	–	–	**Ginger biscuits**
4	–	–	**Glacé cherries**
1 tablespoon	–	–	**Finely chopped peanuts**

METHOD

1.   Break the chocolate into pieces and place it in the pudding basin over the pan of hot water. Stir gently until all the chocolate has melted.

2.   Put the ginger biscuits between two pieces of greaseproof paper and crush with a rolling-pin.

3.   Chop the cherries and stir with the crushed biscuits and the chopped nuts into the melted chocolate. Spoon into small paper sweet cases and leave to set in a cool place.

15. Assorted Sweets

Divinity

Makes approximately 1 ½ lb (675 gm) divinity

EQUIPMENT

1 large heavy saucepan
1 metal tablespoon
1 sugar thermometer
1 egg whisk
1 wooden spoon
1 baking sheet

INGREDIENTS

Imperial	Metric	Cup	Ingredient
2 ½ fl oz	*75 ml*	*⅓*	**Glucose syrup**
¼ teaspoon	*–*	*–*	**Salt**
2 ½ fl oz	*75 ml*	*⅓*	**Water**
18 oz	*500 gm*	*2 ¼*	**Sugar**
2	*–*	*–*	**Egg whites**
1 teaspoon	*–*	*–*	**Vanilla essence**
6 tablespoons	*–*	*–*	**Chopped walnuts**

METHOD

1. Put the glucose syrup, salt, water and sugar into the saucepan and cook over a gentle heat, stirring all the time with the tablespoon until the sugar crystals have dissolved.

2. Bring the dissolved sugar solution to the boil, then reduce the heat to medium, and continue cooking, without stirring, until the temperature reaches 260°F / 127°C.

3. Just before the sugar solution reaches the correct temperature, whisk the egg whites until really stiff and peaky, then pour the hot syrup over the whipped egg whites and continue beating (preferably with an electric hand mixer as this is easier) until the mixture fluffs up.

At this stage add the vanilla essence and continue beating until the mixture loses some of its gloss and holds its shape when dropped from a teaspoon.

4. Fold in the chopped nuts. Use a wooden spoon if the Divinity gets too stiff for the mixer, then swiftly drop teaspoonfuls of the sweet onto a baking sheet lined with waxed paper.

Note:
■ *The Divinity may become a little stiff while you are shaping the first few teaspoonfuls, but if this is the case, add a few drops of hot water and stir well.*

■■ *A quicker method of shaping the Divinity is to*

spoon the mixture into a heavy duty plastic bag or piping bag fitted with a large-plain nozzle. Cut away one corner of the bag and then squeeze small amounts of the Divinity onto the waxed paper. This will give more uniform pieces of sweet.

■■■ *Buy glucose syrup at the chemist's or make by dissolving 8 oz (225 gm / 1 ⅓ cups) glucose in ¼ pt (150 ml / ⅔ cup) water and boil to 230°F / 110°C. Cool and store in an airtight container.*

Peppermint Divinity

1.   Follow recipe and method for Divinity, omitting the chopped walnuts.
2.   Add about ¼ teaspoon oil of peppermint or peppermint extract along with the vanilla essence.
3.   Add a little green food colour.

Divinity Sandwich Layer

1.   Follow recipe and method for Divinity, but boil syrup to 265°F / 129°C.
2.   Instead of shaping it with a teaspoon, pour one half of the mixture into a buttered 1 lb loaf tin or similar sized baking dish, and then fold 4 oz (112 gm) melted plain chocolate into the remaining half and spoon this over the vanilla layer.
3.   When cool and set, chill for 2-3 hours then remove from the pan and cut into about 32 thin slices.

Orange Divinity

1.   Follow recipe and method for Divinity, but omit vanilla essence.
2.   Add either one standard packet of orange-flavoured jelly or 2 tablespoons of jelly crystals then   boil   until 260°F / 127°C is reached.

Note:
■ *If you are using a packet of jelly, first cut it into small pieces with a pair of scissors and then add it to the syrup just before the correct temperature on the sugar thermometer is reached. If you are using the jelly crystals, whisk them in with the egg whites and then continue the recipe as before.*

Lemon Divinity

1.   Follow recipe and method for Divinity, but omit vanilla essence.
2.   Add either one standard pack of lemon-flavoured jelly or 2 tablespoons of lemon-flavoured jelly crystals (see note above) and continue as for Orange Divinity.

Lime Divinity

1.   Follow recipe and method for Divinity, but omit vanilla essence.
2.   Add either one standard packet of lime-flavoured jelly or 2 tablespoons of lime-flavoured jelly crystals (see note above) and continue as for Orange Divinity.

Beige Divinity

1.   Follow recipe and method for Divinity, but instead of using all white sugar, use 9 oz (250 gm / 1 + cups) soft light brown sugar and the same amount of white granulated sugar.
2.   If pecan nuts are available, substitute these for the chopped walnuts.

Divinity Ripple

Makes approximately 1 ½ lb (675 gm) divinity

EQUIPMENT

1 large heavy saucepan
1 metal tablespoon
1 sugar thermometer
1 egg whisk
Waxed paper

INGREDIENTS

Imperial	Metric	Cup	Ingredient
4 fl oz	120 ml	½	*Golden syrup*
4 fl oz	120 ml	½	*Water*
1 lb	450 gm	2	*Granulated sugar*
Pinch	–	–	*Salt*
2	–	–	*Egg whites*
Few drops	–	–	*Vanilla essence*
6 oz	170 gm	–	*Plain chocolate*

METHOD

1.　Put the syrup, water, sugar and salt into the saucepan and cook over a very gentle heat, stirring continuously with the tablespoon until the sugar crystals have dissolved.

2.　Raise the heat until the syrup boils, then reduce it to medium and cook until the thermometer reaches 260°F / 127°C. Do not stir while the mixture is boiling.

3.　Beat the egg whites until really stiff, then pour the hot syrup over them, still beating with an electric or hand whisk.

4.　At this stage add the vanilla essence and continue beating with the mixer or, if the mixture is too stiff, with a wooden spoon until the candy loses some of its gloss and will hold its shape when dropped from a teaspoon.

5.　Very quickly fold in the grated chocolate and then drop teaspoonfuls of the divinity onto waxed paper.

Snow Candy

Makes over 1 lb snow candy

EQUIPMENT

1 large heavy saucepan
1 metal tablespoon
1 sugar thermometer
1 egg whisk
1 wooden spoon

INGREDIENTS

Imperial	Metric	Cup	Ingredient
6 oz	170 gm	¾	**White sugar**
10 oz	280 gm	1 ¾	**Light brown sugar**
2 fl oz	60 ml	¼	**Golden syrup**
4 fl oz	120 ml	½	**Hot water**
Pinch	–	–	**Salt**
2	–	–	**Egg whites**
Few drops	–	–	**Vanilla essence**

Left: A box of peppermint divinity, apple and orange divinity and divinity and sandwich layer

Below: Snow candy, Kerstballen, long box of fruited snow candy and potato candies

METHOD

1. Put the two sorts of sugar, the syrup, hot water and salt into the saucepan. Heat gently, stirring continuously, until the sugar has completely dissolved, then bring to the boil.

2. Reduce the heat to medium and continue cooking at a low boil until the temperature reaches 260°F / 127°C. Remove from the heat.

3. Beat the egg whites until really stiff, then pour the hot syrup over them and continue beating. At this stage add the vanilla essence and beat until the candy loses some of its gloss and holds its shape when dropped from a teaspoon.

4. Drop the finished candy in teaspoonfuls onto waxed paper swirling the teaspoon to make peaks. Leave to set.

Fruited Snow Candy

1. Follow recipe and method for Snow Candy.

2. Fold 4 tablespoons of chopped mixed fruit through the mixture after beating and just before spooning the candy onto the waxed paper.

Nut Snow Candy

1. Follow recipe and method for Snow Candy.

2. Fold 4 tablespoons of finely chopped nuts, hazelnuts, walnuts or almonds through the mixture after beating and just before spooning the candy onto the waxed paper.

Potato Candy

Makes approximately 2 lb (900 gm) candy

EQUIPMENT

1 large mixing bowl
1 sieve
1 wooden spoon
1 damp cloth
1 small basin over a pan of hot water

INGREDIENTS

Imperial	Metric	Cup	Ingredient
3 oz	*80 gm*	*½*	*Mashed potato*
1 teaspoon	*–*	*–*	*Vanilla essence*
¼ teaspoon	*–*	*–*	*Salt*
1 lb	*450 gm*	*3*	*Icing sugar*
6 oz	*170 gm*	*–*	*Chocolate for dipping*
4 oz	*112 gm*	*1*	*Chopped salted peanuts*

METHOD

1. Put the potato, vanilla essence and salt into the mixing bowl, then sift the icing sugar over the potato, stirring in about a quarter of the whole amount each time.

2. As soon as the mixture has the consistency of a stiff dough, knead lightly and cover with a damp cloth. (Add more or less icing sugar for the correct consistency – it should resemble a light scone dough).

3. Chill the dough until it is manageable enough to form into small balls about ½ in (1 ¼ cm) in diameter. Place on a tray and chill again.

4. Melt the chocolate in a small basin over hot water. Dip each candy ball first into the chocolate, then roll in the chopped salted peanuts and leave to set on waxed paper.

Coconut Potato Candies

1. Follow recipe and method for Potato Candy.

2. Add 3 oz (80 gm / 1 cup) desiccated coconut with the icing sugar. Mix in well.

3. Continue as for Potato Candy.

Cherry Krisps

Makes 20 to 30 krisps

EQUIPMENT

1 shallow Swiss roll tin
1 small heavy saucepan
1 wooden spoon
1 sharp knife

INGREDIENTS

Imperial	Metric	Cup	Ingredient
2 oz	56 gm	¼	**Butter**
4 tablespoons	–	–	**Golden syrup**
2 oz	56 gm	⅓	**Soft brown sugar**
4 oz	112 gm	¾	**Icing sugar**
3 oz	80 gm	–	**Rice breakfast cereal**
For decoration	–	–	**Maraschino cherries**

METHOD

1. Put the butter, syrup and brown sugar into the saucepan and heat gently until the butter has melted.

2. Bring to the boil, stirring all the time, then boil the mixture *without stirring* for one minute.

3. Remove the pan from the heat, stir in the icing sugar and cereal and mix well.

4. Turn the mixture into a well buttered Swiss roll tin and leave to set.

5. Cut the set mixture into small squares with a sharp knife and top with a small piece of cherry.

Swiss Crisps

Makes approximately 1 lb (450 gm) crisps

EQUIPMENT

1 large heavy saucepan
1 wooden spoon
1 well greased Swiss roll tin
1 sharp knife

INGREDIENTS

Imperial	Metric	Cup	Ingredient
4 oz	112 gm	½	**Margarine or Butter**
4 oz	112 gm	–	**Marshmallows**
4 oz	112 gm	–	**Home-made or bought toffee**
1 packet	–	–	**Swiss muesli**

METHOD

1. Put the butter or margarine into the saucepan then cut the marshmallows into pieces and add them to the fat. Heat gently.

2. Break the toffee into small pieces and stir it into the marshmallow/fat mixture, continuing to stir over a gentle heat until all the ingredients have melted and combined together.

3. Add sufficient muesli (dry) to make a very stiff dough, then pack this into the greased Swiss roll tin and allow to set.

4. When the mixture is firm cut into pieces or bars and store in an airtight tin until required. To present the crisps, wrap in coloured cellophane paper and serve from an airtight jar.

Kerstballen (Christmas sweets)

Makes approximately 25 sweets

EQUIPMENT

1 small pudding basin
1 pan of hot water
1 mixing bowl
1 large sharp knife
1 wooden chopping board
1 metal teaspoon
1 fork

INGREDIENTS

Imperial	Metric	Cup	Ingredient
1	–	–	**Lemon, juice**
1	–	–	**Green, crisp eating apple**
4 oz	112 gm	¾	**Dried apricots**
6 oz	170 gm	1 ¼	**Plump sultanas**
2 tablespoons	–	–	**Chopped almonds**
1 tablespoon	–	–	**Caster sugar**
6 oz	170 gm	–	**Milk or plain chocolate**

METHOD

1. Squeeze the lemon juice into the mixing bowl, chop the apple into small pieces and toss in the lemon juice.

2. Chop the apricots and sultanas very finely and add these to the chopped apple along.

Right: Sugared almonds and popcorn lollipops

with the chopped nuts and caster sugar. Leave in a cool place for a couple of hours to let the flavours blend together.

3. Break the chocolate into pieces and stand to melt in the pudding basin, over a pan of hot water.

4. Shape the fruit mixture into approximately 25 small balls, then dip them into the melted chocolate, using a fork to lift them out.

5. Tap the fork on the side of the basin to remove excess chocolate, and then gently tip the coated ball onto a sheet of waxed paper. Allow to cool and set.

6. An attractive way of presenting the Kerstballen is to wrap them in thin aluminium foil, making a twist at the top of the sweet. Using a needle and thick thread, attach a short length of cotton to the top of the sweet and use this to tie the Kerstballen onto the Christmas tree.

Dom Rodrigos (Spun Eggs)

Makes approximately 2 lb (900 gm) Spun Eggs

EQUIPMENT

1 large heavy saucepan
1 metal tablespoon
1 egg whisk
1 conical colander
1 large metal draining spoon (with holes)

INGREDIENTS

Imperial	Metric	Cup	Ingredient
1 ¼ lb	560 gm	2 ¼	**Granulated sugar**
1 ½ pt	900 ml	3 ¾	**Water**
8	–	–	**Egg yolks**

METHOD

1. Dissolve the sugar in the water over a low heat (220°F / 104°C), then cook to the consistency of thin honey, stirring continuously with the tablespoon.

2. Beat the egg yolks lightly together, then strain and carefully pour them through the conical strainer into the hot syrup a little at a time. Remove the cooked threads of egg and place them on absorbent paper to drain. These should be eaten within 2 or 3 days of making.

3. To serve, press a few of the egg threads together and place in fluted paper sweet cases.

Walnut Fudgies

Makes approximately 2 lb (900 gm) Fudgies

EQUIPMENT

1 large heavy saucepan
Sugar thermometer
1 wooden spoon
waxed paper
2 teaspoons

INGREDIENTS

Imperial	Metric	Cup	Ingredient
1 lb	450 gm	2	**Granulated sugar**
6 oz	170 gm	1	**Brown sugar**
8 fl oz	240 ml	1	**Water**
½ oz	15 gm	1 tablespoon	**Butter**
12 oz	340 gm	3	**Coarsely chopped walnuts**
¼ teaspoon	–	–	**Salt**

METHOD

1. Mix the sugars with the water and cook to 236°F / 113°C stirring occasionally.

2. Remove the pan from the heat and add the butter, nuts and salt, then beat vigorously until the mixture begins to thicken.

3. Drop onto a sheet of waxed paper, using two teaspoons – one for measuring, one for pushing the candy onto the sheet. Store when cool in an airtight tin.

Sugared Almonds

Makes approximately 2 lb (900 gm) sugared almonds

EQUIPMENT

1 large heavy saucepan
1 metal tablespoon
1 wooden spoon
1 sieve

INGREDIENTS

Imperial	Metric	Cup	Ingredient
1 lb	450 gm	2	**Granulated sugar**
4 fl oz	120 ml	½	**Water**
1 teaspoon	–	–	**Cinnamon**
1 lb	450 gm	3	**Almonds (with skins)**

METHOD

1. Put the sugar and water into the saucepan and dissolve slowly over a low heat, stirring all the time with the tablespoon. Add the cinnamon, stir, raise the heat and then boil until the syrup falls in thick drops from the spoon.

2. Remove from the heat, add the almonds and stir until they are well coated with the syrup. Continue stirring until the syrup dries to sugar. Remove almonds.

3. Put the excess sugar back into the pan, add a little water and dissolve. Boil until the syrup clears, add the once-coated almonds and stir until they are coated a second time with the syrup. Cool and pack in jars with airtight stoppers or lids.

Popcorn Lollipops

Makes approximately 1 lb (450 gm) popcorn

EQUIPMENT

2 large saucepans
2 wooden spoons
1 metal tablespoon
1 large mixing bowl
Wooden lollipop sticks

INGREDIENTS

Imperial	Metric	Cup	Ingredient
2 tablespoons	–	–	**Corn oil**
4 tablespoons	–	–	**Unpopped corn kernels**
6 tablespoons	–	–	**Golden syrup**
4 oz	112 gm	½	**Caster sugar**

METHOD

1. Heat the corn oil in a large saucepan then add the unpopped corn kernels all at once.
2. Cover the saucepan with a lid or piece of aluminium foil and heat over a medium heat until the popping has stopped.
3. Put the corn into a large mixing bowl.
4. Put the syrup and caster sugar into the second saucepan and heat, stirring all the time with the tablespoon, until the sugar has dissolved. Boil for 2 minutes, then pour over the popped corn in the large basin.
5. Mix the corn and syrup until all the pieces of corn are evenly coated, then cool until it can be handled without burning the fingers. Mould into round balls, about the size of a tennis ball and lay on waxed paper to harden. Before the popcorn mixture is completely hard, stick a thin stick into each one so that it can be eaten like a lollipop. Store in an airtight tin. Present wrapped in coloured foil or cellophane.

Left: Walnut fudgies, Swiss crisps, a box of spun eggs and cherry crisps

Glossary

Bloom If chocolates are stored in a place which is too warm or too damp, the surface will become streaked with white. Chocolates are best kept in a cool, dry place.

Blush A term used to describe the pink tinge found on fresh pears, peaches etc. When making marzipan fruits the blush can be obtained by painting the fruit with pink colouring.

Chocolate Vermicelli Small strands of chocolate used for coating truffles etc.

Crust The sugar surface which appears on fondants etc. when they are exposed to the air.

Crystallizing A finish of fine sugar crystals which gives candies an attractive finish and keeps them fresh longer.

Glazing Many sweets such as marzipan shapes, stuffed dates, sugar plums etc. can be given an attractive finish by dipping them or brushing them with a thin sugar syrup – 1 lb sugar (450 gm, 2 cups) to ¼ pt water (150 ml, ⅔ + cup).

Grain When making sweets such as fudge, the hot cooked syrup must be beaten so that tiny sugar crystals form and give the familiar texture of fudge.

Invert Sugar When a little glucose or acid is added to a sugar syrup, it will convert some of the sugar crystals to a simpler molecular structure which will not crystallize so easily when the syrup is boiled.

Kneading Kneading is a process whereby a dough or soft mass of candy (e.g. marzipan) is repeatedly folded and pressed together with the hands until the texture is smooth and even throughout.

Ripen The ripening process is one whereby the flavour and texture of a sweetmeat are left to develop for a short time before the candy is used.

Sugaring Out Sugaring out is a term used to describe the process whereby a fondant becomes a sugary solid – actually a crystallizing process.